Basic
TV Reporting

Ivor Yorke

Focal Press
London and Boston

Focal Press
is an imprint of Butterworth Scientific

 PART OF REED INTERNATIONAL P.L.C.

First published 1990

© **Ivor Yorke, 1990**

British Library Cataloguing in Publication Data

Yorke, Ivor
Basic tv reporting.
   1. Great Britain. News. Reporting by television
   I. Title
   070.430941
   ISBN 0–240–51283–9

Library of Congress Cataloging in Publication Data

Yorke. Ivor.
   Basic TV reporting/Ivor Yorke.
     p. cm.
   Includes bibliographical references.
   ISBN 0–240–51283–9:
   1. Television broadcasting of news
   2. Broadcast journalism—Technique.
   3. Journalism — Technique. I. Title.
   PN4784.T4Y59 1990
   070.1'95—dc20   89-25758

Photoset by TecSet Ltd, Wallington, Surrey
Printed and bound in Great Britain by Courier International
Ltd, Tiptree, Essex

Contents

Acknowledgements

I am particularly grateful to all those who have provided illustrations or helped with picture research in the preparation of this book.

Special thanks therefore to James Feltham and Graham Milloy of BBC Central Stills; Anthony Painter, Picture Editor, Sky; Chris Lambert, Broadcast Developments Ltd, Autoscript; Autocue; Brian Barker, EDS Portaprompt; Hans Rietveld, Key West, Holland; Quantel; Tim Orchard, for trusting me with souvenirs from his US assignments; the International Press Institute for permission to quote from *Journalists on Dangerous Assignments*; Colin Shaw, Director of the Broadcasting Standards Council, for permission to reproduce parts of their draft code; Phil Ashworth and Sarah Finley for acting as models for some of the illustrations.

Thanks too, to those who kindly read through all or part of the manuscript and offered me the benefit of their professional advice: Bernard Hesketh, Mike Scarlett, Tom Wragg, and finally Rob Kirk, Editor of Thames News, who reminded me that while reporting is a serious, responsible and (according to some) a glamorous business, it's also more often than not, a lot of *fun*.

Ivor Yorke

Introduction

Of all the journalists and technicians involved in the production of television news and news-related programmes throughout the world, few if any arouse more interest, controversy and envy than the 'Talent' – those comparative few whose good fortune it is to appear before the public as presenters or reporters.

Ask any aspiring young broadcast journalist for the 'ideal' career, and ten to one he or she will reel off an impressive list of names of those whose exploits they have followed keenly through their reporting from the world's trouble-spots, and whom they would dearly love to emulate given the opportunity. For no matter how strongly it is argued that power and responsibility reside largely with producers and editors, it is difficult to persuade the young not to be dazzled by the glamour of appearing regularly on television in front of millions. The urge to share the same 'front seat on history' that international television reporters take as a normal part of their everyday working lives continues to draw the young and ambitious like a powerful magnet.

Although they may not stop to consider whether they are physically or mentally equipped to undertake such an exacting role, most will at least acknowledge that it is a difficult road, and that reporter styles, just like hair styles, can swiftly go out of fashion for little or no reason. But evidence of the fickleness of the public, let alone that of the executives who run television, rarely succeeds in deflecting any except the faint-hearted. Almost all of the rest simply want to know the price they have to pay for success, and how to get to the front of the queue waiting at the foot of the ladder.

The first thing they need to be told is that many of the most successful television reporters have served an apprenticeship behind the scenes, in print journalism, or in radio, before getting their chance to appear in front of the camera. And while some news organisations are undoubtedly prepared to risk taking on reporters who have no previous experience or training, others insist that potential on-screen talent comes through strictly defined routes which make allowance for careful grooming and instruction along the way.

Not all beginners can expect to have the benefit of that professional education, or indeed of the better college courses which mix the practicalities with the theory. For those, there are hundreds of questions concerned with style, technique and presentation.

This book aims to provide at least some of the answers.

What a Reporter Does

Few of those who aspire to careers as television reporters have more than a vague notion of what the job entails. The work is there on the screen 24 hours a day – but exactly how reporters function, where their responsibilities begin and end, how they link into the editorial chain, and so on, is not so obvious. The public may also be forgiven for confusing the role of reporter with that of anchor/newscaster/newsreader/presenter, because the roles sometimes overlap. Reporting may indeed be seen as a natural stepping-stone to the safety and warmth of the studio, but once installed as part of the news-processing as opposed to news-gathering team, reporters are usually less originators of their own material than shapers of other people's.

Origins of television journalism
Once you become a television journalist you join a young profession with its roots chiefly in newspapers, magazines and radio. It can be a confusing world: those who work in it cannot quite bring themselves to admit that they are part of show business, and many job titles suggest a lingering bond with print journalism. So subeditors, copytasters, editors, reporters and correspondents are still to be found alongside scriptwriters, producers, directors and presenters.

Written news stories are called 'scripts' not 'copy'.

Reporting responsibilities
The role you have to fulfil depends entirely on your employer. In some organisations television reporters are treated separately as specialists: in others they are expected to double up as camera operators or picture editors. Yet although the title may cover any or all of these duties, what usually distinguishes 'reporters' from all other journalists in television is that they 'get the story'. This is likely to mean taking editorial responsibility for the content, shape and eventual coherence of an entire television report – assessing on the spot the newsworthiness of an event and the people in it, carrying out interviews, performing a piece to camera and writing voice-over commentary, as well as co-ordinating the activities of the camera crew. You may also have to attend to the logistics of meeting deadlines. No 'Brownie points' are won for a brilliant piece of work which arrives too late for inclusion in the programme for which it was intended.

But don't imagine that you will spend all your working life on the road. You will be newsroom-bound for a large proportion of the time, engaged in tracking down story leads, writing scripts, or providing the voice-over for incoming agency pictures or compilations. You are also likely to be called on to conduct live studio interviews, where the emphasis is on an ability to perform rather like a circus trapeze artist – without a safety net.

1. Conducts research on the spot

2. Decides content and shape

3. Supervises camera crew

4. Carries out interviews

5. Does piece to camera

6. Writes and records voice-over

7. Maintains base links

What a reporter does
In the field reporters are in charge of covering stories as the representatives of
their programmes or news organisations. Responsibility includes management of
the camera team as well as control of editorial content.

13

The TV reporter is part of a team.

A Place on the Taxi Rank

Unless yours is a small organisation where reporters are expected to be 'self-starters' providing all their own ideas, your first responsibility as a newcomer will be to that part of the operation dealing with news gathering. Intake/input/the assignments desk/news desk decides which events are worthy of coverage and assigns staff to cover them. The 'desk' controls your reporting life on behalf of the news editor, who is also likely to give you experience of intake work by assigning you to act as a stand-in occasionally.

The predictability of news
News is a far more predictable phenomenon than it may seem, and a large proportion of every news-related programme appears as a result of good intelligence about events before they take place. Advance information on matters both routine and important flows never-endingly into the head-quarters of every news organisation from a myriad of official and un-official sources, to form the basis of a diary from which conventional daily programmes are constructed. The unexpected nature of the rest of the news means that reporters are sometimes matched with stories simply as they arise. Not for nothing is the reporters' room sometimes known as the 'taxi rank'.

Correspondents, in effect more senior reporters, may have more of a roving commission and so exercise greater influence on the coverage of events not on the diary. Other news-related programmes, whose commit-ments may be over longer periods, operate very differently. Here the reporter may be part of a team involved in researching items, or may be contracted to provide an acceptable voice and face at the conclusion of a detailed planning process carried out by others.

In the field
If you have worked in newspapers or radio you will probably have operated alone. As a television reporter you are one of a team. Although the tendency is towards smaller crews, current working practices still lean towards the requirement for a camera operator, a sound recordist, and possibly a lighting assistant or electrician to set up and supervise a portable lighting rig. Sometimes the reporter may be joined by a field producer/director acting as a link with the camera crew.

Editing
Your responsibility for covering a news item, once completed, usually passes along the editorial chain to the picture editors, who assemble the pictures and sound into the proper order for transmission. Sometimes you may be expected to supervise this work; otherwise it is a producer or programme editor who makes decisions about content and duration. (See page 94.)

14

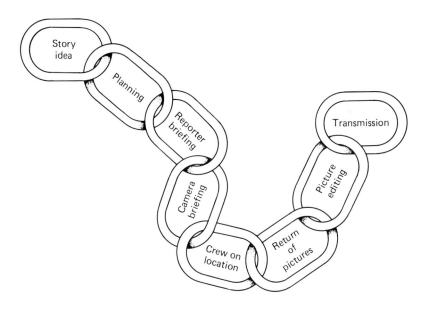

The editorial chain
The reporter represents a single link in the editorial chain, which begins with the idea for a story and ends with its transmission as part of a programme. Most news-related programmes split editorial responsibilities. Reporters belong to one group of journalists (intake/input/assignments) devoted to gathering the news. The other (output) processes and prepares the material for broadcast.

What Makes a Good Reporter

What makes a good reporter for television is what makes a good journalist in any other medium, only more so.

The forces which drive most who embark on a career in the profession – a 'nose' for news, born scepticism, hunger for truth and knowledge, and the desire to communicate – have to be weighed against qualities of a more physically obvious nature. At the minimum these consist of a reasonable appearance and a voice of acceptable broadcast standard (see page 42). More than that you will need to develop a thick skin, a touch of arrogance, and the determination not to be deterred by the number of other news people who congregate at the scene of important events.

Persistence...and sensitivity

Do not expect to be able to hide in the crowd and still succeed, because no television organisation involved in the business of topical journalism could live for long with the regular failure of their man or woman to visibly get the story. The nature of the job is inherently high-profile, so it is sometimes necessary to push through the scrum to get the interview. Quotes cannot be invented for the camera.

In contrast, the good television reporter is expected to know intuitively how to react in situations which call for sensitivity and thoughtfulness. There must be tact, sympathy and an ability to recognise when the moment has come to withdraw discreetly from pursuit of a story in which, say, lives have been lost.

A love of language

It is taken for granted that every would-be journalist can write. The ability to spell is thought by some not to be as important. What is not in doubt is that good reporters should have a natural feel for language, an instinct for the right word at the right time. But since most television insists that its precious air time is not wasted, the pressure is on to produce material which is disciplined, spare and economical. The salient points of every item must be marshalled sensibly and coherently, the language stripped to its bare bones and put to work alongside the pictures.

An eye for illustration

Although it is the camera team's responsibility to gather the pictures, the good reporter develops an understanding of the visual element. The golden rule is that words and pictures must go together. Divergence leads to competition between the two, distracting the audience. In that case, picture-power will always win.

What makes a good reporter
Patience and persistence are part of a reporter's make-up, but in the scrimmage which is a regular part of world news gathering, no-one can afford to be left behind by the competition. The world's press at their vigil (1) outside the London hospital where the Duchess of York gave birth to her first child, Princess Beatrice, in August 1988 (author's photo) and (2) at the site of the British Midland air-crash near the M1 motorway, January 1989 (courtesy BBC Central Stills)

The Reporter as Manager

It will not be long before a professional camera unit working on any news-type programme consists of no more than two people – a reporter and a single technician. Until that becomes standard practice, knowing how to be an effective team leader will remain an integral part of the reporter's job, as being in charge of the camera crew usually goes with editorial responsibility for the story. Strong-willed professionals inevitably have differences of opinion from time to time, making 'management' a daunting prospect, but even as a newcomer you must always be assertive, take the lead and set the pace. At all times know what you want, because inexperienced or contract crews will expect to follow instructions – sometimes to the letter.

Reporter–crew relationship

Because the creation of every television report is the combination of creative processes, a positive working relationship between reporter and crew is far more likely to produce successful results than one in which members of the team are at odds with each other. In some circumstances how far you are united in your determination to pursue a news story could make the difference between life and death.

Trust and interdependability work both ways. Nothing damns a reporter more quickly in the eyes of the crew than cocksureness and unreliability, especially a failure to get to a location on time. Remember, too, how important it is to keep the crew informed. Say clearly what you expect from them, and although it is not necessary for you to know the technical details of every piece of equipment, a rudimentary understanding of and interest in how things work will contribute towards telling the story.

Meeting deadlines

Before satellites and microwave links became commonplace, news programmes relied on more basic forms of communication to ensure that their material got back to base in time for editing and transmission. The principle, if not the means, remains the same. If anything, deadlines have shrunk, increasing pressure on the team in the field – the reporter especially – to plan their mission down to the finest detail. Calculations about the time needed to travel to and from the scene of a story, to gather the pictures and judge their worth, to shape the material on the spot or to send raw rushes to be edited at home base, plus a safety margin, have to be built into the schedule if programme requirements are to be met.

The whole process has been speeded up with the introduction of mobile picture-editing suites and satellite news-gathering facilities which allow news teams to dispense with the use of local television stations, but the ability to control the logistical problems involved in reporting is valued almost as much as editorial talent.

18

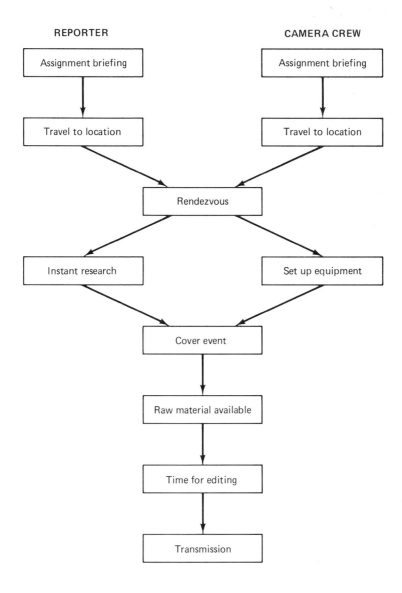

REPORTER	CAMERA CREW
Assignment briefing	Assignment briefing
Travel to location	Travel to location

Rendezvous

| Instant research | Set up equipment |

Cover event

Raw material available

Time for editing

Transmission

Managing a news story
Whatever the assignment, you must make a conscious effort to ensure all stages are completed so the material reaches your base – by whatever means – in time for it to be transmitted as part of the programme for which it is intended. Allow sufficient leeway for your story to be edited on the spot or for the 'rushes' to be assembled elsewhere. Always build in a safety margin, especially when operating abroad.

19

Don't let all your news be 'second hand'.

Thinking about News

It needs no special talent to be able to recognise a conventional, 'big' news story when it occurs. Political change, social upheaval, sporting achievement, natural disaster – each event speaks loudly for itself. What distinguishes the journalist from the rest is a well-honed ability to identify the subjects which, although less obvious, stimulate interest or have real bearing on people's lives.

Beyond McLurg

A commonly held view is that television journalism offers a severely limited view of society, and a parochial one at that. Some sociologists call it 'The Gate', an inevitable byproduct of the upbringing, education and social attitudes of those in the profession. Others maintain that the news agenda was determined long ago by newspaper journalism and that television has always lacked the will and resources to break the mould.

It is up to you and every other reporter to try to broaden the agenda, even if it means questioning received wisdoms, one of which holds that the importance of an event diminishes with its distance from your own doorstep. (This phenomenon is sometimes whimsically known as McLurg's Law after the senior editor who first recognised it.) As a result, matters of potentially real significance to humanity are ignored and whole swathes of the world go under-reported until countries about which little has been heard for years suddenly become the centre of attention.

Equally, subjects for news coverage rapidly fall in and out of fashion for no apparent reason. Viewers become bored with the same 'running story' week after week, however important it may be. As a contrast, issues which once scarcely merited mention, chiefly because they seemed too difficult to illustrate, become exposed to prolonged treatment. Thus, as the century draws to a close, Economics and Environment are in, Sunday routine Protest and the Falling Chimney syndrome (virtually) out.

Differences in news values

Television and newspaper journalists differ widely in their attitudes towards news. The tabloid press will frequently splash their front pages with offbeat or bizarre stories ignored by the more serious newspapers. Television will sometimes kick off with picture items which have little relevance for either print or sound. So how does anyone assess what is news?

- First, always ask yourself how valuable it is to the audience.
- Scouring the newspapers for stories to follow up is a poor substitute for your own ideas.
- Do not sit back and wait to be spoon-fed by what pours off the agency wire services.
- Get as close to the grass roots as possible in an attempt to generate original material.

20

Thinking about the news
Journalists differ widely in their attitudes. Newspapers aim their content at known socio-economic groups and don't rate subjects to which others give high priority.

21

Understanding Television

No journalist newcomer to television is expected to be an expert in electronics, but a basic understanding of the technical principles behind equipment is bound to be useful. We take a television picture for granted: but how many applicants for a reporter's job would be able to explain how a picture is received?

A single television picture is made up of horizontal lines which appear on the receiver in rapid succession from left to right, top to bottom. The lines are transmitted in two sequential 'fields'. In the European 625-line picture, for example, the first 312.5 odd numbered-lines are followed by a second field made up of 312.5 even-numbered lines. The two fields are interlaced to reduce flicker, doubling the effective number of 'pictures' seen per second.

The more lines, the more defined the picture, hence the move towards HDTV (High Definition Television) which in any of its developing rival systems would give over a thousand lines, offering brilliant clarity on bigger screens.

Colour
Colour pictures are based on a mixture of red, green and blue light. Every image captured by the lens is broken down into these three primary colours. Inside the camera they meet correspondingly coloured picture tubes coated with light-sensitive dots. An electron gun at the back of each tube scans the coating, triggering a stream of electrons which are turned into an electronic signal. The three signals, one for each tube, are then combined to re-create the picture.

CCD (Charged-Coupled Device) cameras don't use tubes at all but have 'chips' to convert the red, green and blue light into electrical signals.

Teletext
No modern television system needs every one of the lines for carrying picture signals, and since the mid-1970s use has been made of some of the blank ones to broadcast Teletext, a method allowing information to appear on the screen as 'pages' of written text and graphics. Current practice is to string these pages together in the form of 'magazines' made up of news, sport, weather, financial information, travel, entertainment and so on. Access to each page is through a remote-controlled keypad roughly the size of an electronic calculator.

Satellite and cable
Under normal atmospheric conditions television picture signals are transmitted by microwaves travelling in straight lines over short distances. Long-range transmission is achieved by sending the signals into space, where they are received by orbiting communications satellites and then directed back towards ground stations on earth. The system has been

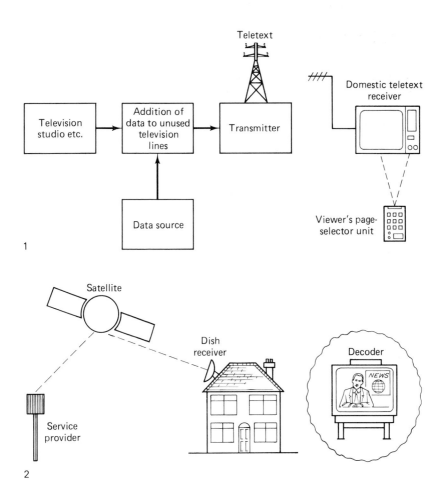

1

2

Broadcasting developments

Teletext (1) has offered a new concept in broadcasting information since the 1970s. Information carried as part of the television signal appears on the screen as 'pages' of information. Teletext is also used for subtitling and data transmission, and the latest systems can send multiple-language text and high-quality still pictures. DBS (2), heralding a television revolution through tiny dish aerials, offers a wide range of news and entertainment to viewers, and jobs for television reporters.

refined to the point where the signal can be beamed to individual homes equipped with small dish aerials. This development is known as DBS (Direct Broadcasting by Satellite).

Cable television has been available since the 1940s, bringing signals to areas facing geographical difficulties or distances from transmitters. Modern subscribers benefit from a wide choice of existing and new services.

Futures

Laypeople are commonly under the impression that 'news' consists entirely of unexpected and spectacular happenings in all parts of the world. This is not the case. Nor do television reporters go roaming the streets with their camera crews in search of news: it would be time-consuming and almost entirely non-productive. News gathering has to be approached on an organised and systematic basis. Professionally organised news services recognise this by dedicating teams of journalists to the filtering and discussion of ideas, building a catalogue of scheduled events at home and abroad from which entries will be plucked for possible coverage.

This planning or futures desk – cornerstone of the intake or input department – is responsible for noting the dates of Parliamentary sessions, anniversaries, court sittings, the publication of official documents, and a wide range of other events which may be considered worthy of treatment by television.

Planners scour every newspaper and magazine that comes their way (the more obscure the better), watch other television programmes, listen to the radio, listen to gossip and rumour, and cultivate anyone who might provide a tip-off to a news story, in an effort to assemble the widest possible agenda from which a choice can be made.

The flow is two ways. Invitations to attend events are issued, facilities offered. On other occasions permission may have to be sought for reporters and camera crews to join private or public occasions, and then it is a matter of obtaining entry passes, security clearances or whatever documentation is required for access. Some really big events are arranged years in advance, and news organisations spend considerable time and effort to ensure they are represented, and have access to the proper communications and facilities.

Foreign news

Coverage of foreign news requires special attention, especially when reporters are assigned from their home base to cover stories. They may not be allowed to enter another country without a visa applied for several weeks ahead, and permission may have to be sought to take in a camera crew, customs declarations prepared, and official accreditation sought, all of which may take frustratingly long to arrange.

Regrettably few countries allow complete freedom of access to their own journalists, let alone to outsiders, and it is not unknown for planners to spend months unsuccessfully wooing those with the power to sanction such a visit. Quite often it is not so much what is happening in a country which is of interest to the outside world – simply that a closed or secretive society is for some reason prepared to open its doors briefly.

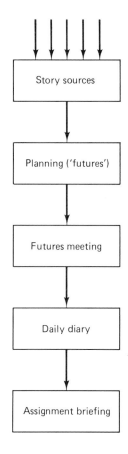

Pathway to the news
Story ideas for consideration follow an established route. Even those programmes or organisations with limited resources try to devote staff to essential planning duties. Any relationship between affiliated, local or regional television or radio stations multiplies sources and adds to news-gathering efficiency. Where radio and television operate side by side or in a genuine 'bi-media' environment, reporters may at times be called on to work in either discipline.

Assignment Planning

The second part of the planners' task is to assemble the list of story possibles into a suitable form for discussion at senior editorial level. These meetings are usually held at weekly or monthly intervals, the aim being to give programme editors sufficient time in which to evaluate everything being suggested. Some items are quickly discarded, others referred back for further investigation before a decision is reached. For those that get the go-ahead, logistical problems may be considered briefly – perhaps the need for special travel arrangements, satellite bookings, co-operation with other departments or organisations – before detailed planning gets under way.

As a reporter you might not be involved at this early stage. It depends on the way your organisation works, whether news planning and news processing are separate or combined, and what ideas you have fed into the system.

The daily diary

Once reduced to manageable and unfanciful proportions, the original list of possibles becomes a declaration of commitment known as 'the diary' or 'the prospects', issued at the start of each working day. Now begins the detailed organisation of every story – at first sight a simple enough task, in reality often a slow, painstaking, frustrating experience. A planner's typical day might run thus:

● Arrange the collection of a long-awaited government publication in time for you to read, digest and turn into an item for the main news.

● Ensure that you and a camera crew, arriving separately from other duties, rendezvous at the same entrance of a building where an important interviewee can spare you exactly ten minutes.

● Find an official with the authority to open a security gate to allow the camera crew to drive within a short distance of where they need to set up their equipment.

This may seem to add up to a series of tedious chores far removed from journalism. But without it the document may not be read properly and an important angle missed; you and the crew may kick your heels at different entrances while the interviewee gives up and goes on to his next appointment without seeing you; the crew may have to carry their equipment half a mile from the public car park.

The assignments desk

Responsibility now shifts from the planners to the assigners – sometimes the same people, sometimes not. Reporters with known subject expertise are invariably allocated stories which make use of it. Briefing ranges from the cursory – not much more than subject heading, location and the name of a 'contact' – to the detailed discussion of treatment, content and the questions to be asked of interviewees.

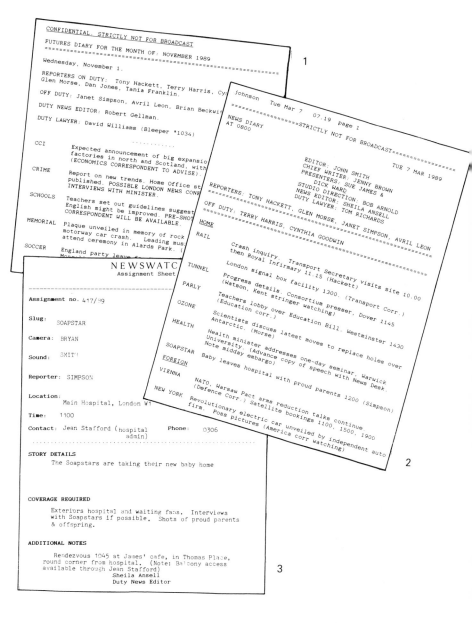

Document 1:

==
FUTURES DIARY FOR THE MONTH OF: NOVEMBER 1989
==
Wednesday, November 1.

REPORTERS ON DUTY: Tony Hackett, Terry Harris, Cy[...]
Glen Morse, Dan Jones, Tania Franklin.

OFF DUTY: Janet Simpson, Avril Leon, Brian Beckwi[...]

DUTY NEWS EDITOR: Robert Gellman.

DUTY LAWYER: David Williams (Bleeper *1034)

....

CCI   Expected announcement of big expansio[...]
          factories in north and Scotland, with[...]
          (ECONOMICS CORRESPONDENT TO ADVISE).

CRIME   Report on new trends. Home Office st[...]
          published. POSSIBLE LONDON NEWS CONF[...]
          INTERVIEWS WITH MINISTER.

SCHOOLS   Teachers set out guidelines suggest[...]
          English might be improved. PRE-SHO[...]
          CORRESPONDENT WILL BE AVAILABLE.

MEMORIAL Plaque unveiled in memory of rock[...]
          motorway car crash.   Leading mus[...]
          attend ceremony in Alards Park. ([...]

SOCCER   England party leave [...]

Document 2:

Johnson   Tue Mar 7   07.19   Page 1
===
NEWS DIARY ==========STRICTLY NOT FOR BROADCAST==========
AT 0800

                         EDITOR: JOHN SMITH   TUE 7 MAR 1989
                         CHIEF WRITER: JENNY BROWN
                         PRESENTERS: SUE JAMES &
                              DICK WARD
                         STUDIO DIRECTION: BOB ARNOLD
REPORTERS: TONY HACKETT, GLEN MORSE, JANET SIMPSON, AVRIL LEON
                         NEWS EDITOR: SHEILA ANSELL
                         DUTY LAWYER: TOM RICHARDS
==
OFF DUTY: TERRY HARRIS, CYNTHIA GOODWIN
==

HOME

RAIL   Crash inquiry. Transport Secretary visits site 10.00
          then Royal Infirmary 11.15 (Hackett)

TUNNEL   London signal box facility 1300. (Transport Corr.)

PARLY   Progress details. Consortium presser, Dover 1145
          (Watson, Kent stringer watching)

OZONE   Teachers lobby over Education Bill. Westminster 1430
          (Education corr.)

HEALTH   Scientists discuss latest moves to replace holes over
          Antarctic. (Morse)

SOAPSTAR Health minister addresses one-day seminar, Warwick
          University. (Advance copy of speech with News Desk.
FOREIGN   Note midday embargo)

VIENNA   Baby leaves hospital with proud parents 1200 (Simpson.

NEW YORK NATO, Warsaw Pact arms reduction talks continue.
          (Defence Corr.) Satellite bookings 1100, 1500, 1900
          Revolutionary electric car unveiled by independent auto
          firm. Poss pictures (America corr watching)

Document 3:

NEWSWATC[...]
Assignment Sheet

Assignment no. 417/89

Slug: SOAPSTAR

Camera: BRYAN

Sound: SMITH

Reporter: SIMPSON

Location:
           Main Hospital, London W1

Time: 1100

Contact: Jean Stafford (hospital   Phone: 0306
                          admin)
....
STORY DETAILS
     The Soapstars are taking their new baby home

COVERAGE REQUIRED

     Exteriors hospital and waiting fans. Interviews
     with Soapstars if possible. Shots of proud parents
     & offspring.

ADDITIONAL NOTES

     Rendezvous 1045 at James' cafe, in Thomas Place,
     round corner from hospital. (Note: Balcony access
     available through Jean Stafford)
                    Sheila Ansell
                    Duty News Editor

Story planning
Not all news is about unexpected events. Detailed planning of known
happenings is carried out well ahead. 'Futures' information (1) is distilled into
Daily Diaries (2). The Assignment Sheet (3) provides a basic briefing for reporter
and camera crew.

Sources

Television news-related organisations are overwhelmed with unsolicited information which pours in from members of the public and with every mail delivery. In some cases it provides the backbone for programme coverage, but for the rest, existence without resort to some consistent professional back-up is likely to be regarded as scarcely possible.

The agencies
Much of the raw material on which news programmes are based comes fresh from the national and international wire services. Reuters, the Associated Press (AP), United Press International (UPI), Agence France Press (AFP) and others like them provide a valuable subscription service of reports which appear on the teleprinters and – increasingly – the video screens in newsrooms all over the world. Agency staff and freelance reporters are often the first to break stories, setting the pace for others to follow if they please.

Nearer home, each news desk has its own trusted sources to supplement the flow of intelligence from which the diaries are built up. The individual reporter – particularly the specialist – has the contacts book.

Making contact
People make news – so the name, address and telephone number of anyone who is or is ever likely to be of the slightest professional use should never be discarded. Those you come across may be previous interviewees, potential interviewees or providers of fact, record or opinion. Make a note of the officials of organisations which issue invitations or publicity handouts, local politicians and celebrities. Minor officials become major ones. Local politicians become national figures. Do not forget the expertise which is bound to exist within your own circle of friends, or the organisations to which you belong. Keep headed notepaper or visiting cards containing useful names and addresses.

Correspondence columns are also useful sources. A large proportion of letters comes from those who represent organisations of all types, and a surprising number of well-known people who hesitate to list their telephone numbers openly include their addresses when writing to newspapers. Keep a record of all those who might be of use.

Starting from scratch takes time, so at first it might be worth considering sharing names with others. Start by swapping with a colleague of similar status. If you each concentrate on one subject area at a time you will make double the progress in half the time.

Keeping the list
Lastly, when you have built up your list, keep it safely. Experienced reporters guard their contacts books jealously. It may be worth putting yours in the bank when you go on holiday.

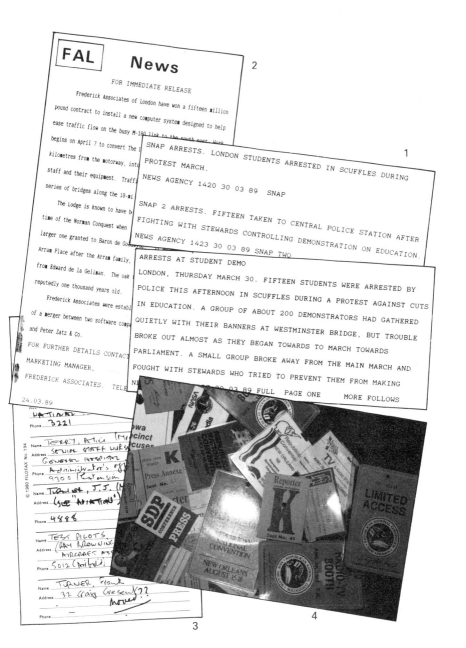

FAL News

FOR IMMEDIATE RELEASE

Frederick Associates of London have won a fifteen million pound contract to install a new computer system designed to help ease traffic flow on the busy M-180 link to the south east. Work begins on April 7 to convert The L... ...kilometres from the motorway, into ...staff and their equipment. Traff... ...series of bridges along the 18-mi...

The Lodge is known to have b... time of the Norman Conquest when ... larger one granted to Baron de Go... Arram Place after the Arram family, ... from Edward de la Gellman. The oak ... reputedly one thousand years old.

Frederick Associates were establi... of a merger between two software comp... and Peter Zatz & Co.

FOR FURTHER DETAILS CONTAC... MARKETING MANAGER, FREDERICK ASSOCIATES. TEL...

24.03.89

SNAP ARRESTS. LONDON STUDENTS ARRESTED IN SCUFFLES DURING PROTEST MARCH.

NEWS AGENCY 1420 30 03 89   SNAP

SNAP 2 ARRESTS. FIFTEEN TAKEN TO CENTRAL POLICE STATION AFTER FIGHTING WITH STEWARDS CONTROLLING DEMONSTRATION ON EDUCATION.

NEWS AGENCY 1423 30 03 89 SNAP TWO

ARRESTS AT STUDENT DEMO

LONDON, THURSDAY MARCH 30. FIFTEEN STUDENTS WERE ARRESTED BY POLICE THIS AFTERNOON IN SCUFFLES DURING A PROTEST AGAINST CUTS IN EDUCATION. A GROUP OF ABOUT 200 DEMONSTRATORS HAD GATHERED QUIETLY WITH THEIR BANNERS AT WESTMINSTER BRIDGE, BUT TROUBLE BROKE OUT ALMOST AS THEY BEGAN TOWARDS TO MARCH TOWARDS PARLIAMENT. A SMALL GROUP BROKE AWAY FROM THE MAIN MARCH AND FOUGHT WITH STEWARDS WHO TRIED TO PREVENT THEM FROM MAKING

...30 03 89 FULL   PAGE ONE   MORE FOLLOWS

3

4

Sources

The wire services often provide the first indication of a breaking story (1), although much news coverage is prearranged. Unsolicited publicity handouts sometimes contain information (2) worthy of being followed up. Good reporters build their own contacts and guard them jealously (3). Detailed planning for and entry to occasions of national and international importance takes time, effort and the right credentials (4).

Making Use of Your Contacts

Gossip and rumour are no substitute for fact, so it doesn't do to believe everything you are told. Scepticism is healthy as long as it does not become obsessive and blind you to accepting the evidence of your own eyes and ears.

The double-check

Contacts who seek you out may be genuinely anxious to help or may have their own axes to grind. It happens. If in doubt cross-check with other sources. Keep faith with your informants and respect their confidentiality if that is what they wish. Some reporters have gone to prison rather than reveal their sources of information. But be careful. Do not make promises you cannot keep. In some circumstances the act of receiving information can in itself be regarded as being in contravention of the law.

Briefings and lobbies

Reporters who deal with specialist subjects usually operate in groups which enjoy some privileges denied to generalists. Advance copies of official reports, speeches and other documents are made available to assist full and accurate reporting. Security passes and identity cards are issued to reporters with official accreditation.

Members of the White House Press Corps, for example, are given facilities to report Presidential activities. Aides give regular briefings – i.e. government or Presidential views on the state of the world or other issues of the day. Where the President goes, so does the resident Press Corps. The lobby system in Britain enables political journalists to meet senior politicians and officials on a regular 'non-attributable' basis (see panel opposite), bringing with it the opportunity to discover current government thinking.

Uses and abuses

Although they have their uses, these systems are open to abuse. 'Lobbies' allow government officials or ministers to use the press to float ideas or theories which may not be official policy, and controversy over what has or has not been said at such meetings (which are never supposed to take place) has begun to lead to the discrediting of the whole idea.

Yet those who are barred from entry or refuse to take part sometimes find themselves at a disadvantage. Some stories are impossible to cover properly without 'official' help. Miss the plane to the President's next destination and you miss the story. You cannot buy a ticket to a remote war zone, so you have to enlist the help of the military to get you there and provide access to communications.

The trouble is that you will be taken subject to conditions imposed by your hosts – and in some cases that might be thought too high a price to pay.

30

Birmingham City University – Kenrick Library
Self Service Receipt for items borrowed

Title: Basic tv reporting
Item: 6107439385
Due: 02/12/2009 23:59

Total items: 1
28/10/2009 19:42

Week loan items CANNOT be renewed.

ON THE RECORD means what you are told is for broadcast or publication.
• No problem, subject to legal constraints.

OFF THE RECORD means what you are told is not for broadcast or publication.
• More of a problem. Try to establish in advance how much of the information you *can* use. Don't agree to the condition retrospectively without very serious consideration.

NOT FOR ATTRIBUTION means you can broadcast or publish what you are told as long as you do not reveal the source of the information.
• Very much a problem. Sometimes used in an attempt at news management. Be wary.

LOBBY BRIEFINGS are usually for groups of specialist journalists by invitation from government or other official sources. Information may by given only on a non-attributable basis.
• Can be a problem. If you join a lobby you must expect to abide by its rules.

ACCREDITATION gives limited numbers of journalists access to places or events where official information is made available.
• Ditto. Being accredited is sometimes the only way of getting to a story.

EMBARGOES allow journalists to have advance copies of documents, reports, speeches or other information on the understanding that broadcast or publication will not take place until a given time.
• Useful but sometimes contentious. Treat every embargo on its merits and be alert to the possibility of news manipulation. Always check advance copies of speeches against delivery: there is no guarantee against a speaker departing from a prepared text.

NEWS BLACKOUTS are sought by the authorities when they believe broadcast or publication could endanger life.
• Acceptable only under certain conditions usually decided at high level. Never commit yourself. Always refer such requests to senior colleagues.

REQUESTS FOR ANONYMITY are made by people who believe broadcast or publication would be harmful.
• Treat with caution. There are circumstances in which anonymity should be granted: make no promises and refer to senior colleagues.

Take the time to watch others at work.

Seven Days of Self-training (1)

This suggested pattern is intended to provide a basis for understanding how a reporter fits into a news organisation. As every television station is structured differently, no more than a general guide can be offered, so adapt the programme to suit your own circumstances.

Try to carry out all stages over a concentrated period of a week, but if this is not possible, follow through on successive off-duty days. The programme assumes the willingness of others to let you observe them at work. If you are invited to make a practical contribution so much the better, but remember your chief purpose is to learn from others.

Day 1: Planning and assignments
Sit with those responsible for sifting through ideas for coverage. Helping to answer the telephone or open the mail will give you a feel for the range of material which comes up for consideration. Judge for yourself what is newsworthy and compare the decisions taken by those doing the job for real. Go to planning meetings which discuss the details of home and foreign assignments. See how stories are graded in importance and the depth of briefing reporters are given before they embark on a project. Listen to the communications between reporters in the field and editors back at base. Assess the accuracy, quality, frequency and amount of information on offer. If necessary, determine to improve it when your turn comes.

Day 2: On the road
Accompany a reporter and camera crew on assignment, preferably one which needs thought and careful planning rather than a straight hard news story requiring little finesse. Stay and observe until the end, no matter how tedious it might become. Make a note of the order in which the reporter tackles the various ingredients, and how well or badly he or she treats interviewees, contacts or others involved. In particular watch closely for the personal/professional relationship between reporter and camera team. It will provide a valuable yardstick against which to measure your own future approach.

Day 3: Picture editing
Follow 'your' story into the editing suite and watch the picture editor assembling it. If possible spend time with more than one editor; get an idea of their routines and contrast their styles. Is one a quicker worker than others? What shots are they inclined to discard? Are they led by the strength of the pictures or the sound? Do they slavishly follow instructions or do they use their imagination? At what point, if any, does editorial supervision take place?

Day 1:
Planning and
assignments
(courtesy BBC
Central Stills)

Day 2:
On the road
(courtesy
Sky News)

Day 3:
Picture
editing

Self-training (1)
Using spare time to watch what happens at each stage will provide a valuable insight into the editorial process and help you develop your own approach to working relationships.

Seven Days of Self-training (2)

The second part of the seven-day self-training programme concentrates on production and technical areas.

Day 4: Graphics
Follow the activities of one graphics designer over the course of the whole day. Is one programme served, or are there several 'customers', each requiring a different style? Make sure you understand the system. Is instruction given verbally, or is there a more formal procedure? Are ideas for graphics generated by reporters or other journalists for the artist to follow, or vice versa? Time how long it takes to create each graphic and note the periods of the day when pressure of work seems greatest. Ask who is responsible for checking the accuracy of graphics designs – particularly figures and spellings – against original ideas and completed scripts. On transmission, make a particular point of judging whether there is a real match between the graphic and the accompanying commentary. If there is little or none, find out why.

Day 5: The newsroom
Observe a newswriter or item producer at work on your chosen programme and monitor every stage of the process. Get an idea of what sources are used, particularly those which are considered reliable and those which are not. Note how much of the script is the writer's own words and how much is a straight crib from wire copy. Pay special attention to the writer's working relationships with programme editor, reporter and picture editor working on the same story, and how much influence is brought to bear by others. Be there when the running order/rundown is constructed. Try to understand why items are shortened or dropped. Stay for the programme post mortem, if there is one.

Day 6: Studio and production
Follow the studio director as preparations are made to put the programme on the air. Sit in on script or technical conferences and listen to what is said about journalistic performances. Watch the rehearsal, however sketchy it might be. Evaluate the director's performance under the pressure of a live newscast. Spend some time in the studio, where you can judge whether the floor manager gives clear signals and whether the script-prompting operation is effective.

Day 7: Practice
By the time you have reached Day 7 your colleagues will have decided you are a perfectionist or a plain nuisance. Either way, persuade them to give you some reading practice during studio downtime. A script from a previous transmission will suffice. Use the electronic prompting device, if there is one. Then ask for an honest opinion.

Day 4: Graphics
(courtesy Quantel)

Day 5: Newsroom
(courtesy
Sky News)

Day 6: Production
(courtesy BBC
Central Stills)

Day 7: Practice
(courtesy EDS
Portaprompt)

Self-training (2)
The second half of the programme concentrates on production and technical
areas. You should end up with a full understanding of how your organisation
works and the part you will play in it.

35

Develop interest in a specialist subject.

Making the Most of Your Talent

Television reporters are expected to be bright, eager, inquisitive and persistent. These are the minimum qualities you should already possess before even beginning to develop 'performing' skills for the screen. Nothing can be achieved without them so make sure they come across – to your programme editor, to those you deal with every day in the pursuit of your journalism and, above all, to your audience. Understand every story before you embark on it. Make use of the 'cuttings' and any other material which might prove useful. Think. Be informed: there is nothing worse than a reporter who is made to look foolish by an interviewee because of his own ignorance. It may seem obvious, but read the newspapers and magazines. Watch television, especially your own output and your closest competition. Listen to radio journalism. If possible learn some of its basic techniques: they could come in useful. Become proficient in shorthand and typing or word-processing – tools of the trade. Learn to drive, if that is appropriate for where you intend to work. Be interested in everything from sport to politics. Learn another language. Who knows when it will lead to a glamorous foreign assignment?

Style and 'presence'
The qualities which add up to a good screen 'presence' are in themselves almost impossible to define. It is easier to identify the negative. The camera is a cruel exposer of physical peculiarities and mannerisms, and the microphone exaggerates speech defects. Even so, every editor has a different idea of what personality is suitable for his or her programme. Voice and looks also come into it because, like it or not, there is no escaping human nature. But a pretty or handsome face is not enough. Fashions change, sometimes driven by the technology which creates the demand for different skills.

At one time television news seemed to be peopled entirely by solemn, mature males with greying hair. Then came an explosion in the opportunities for women. The biggest change of all has seen the replacement of the news 'reader' by the news 'presenter' or news 'caster', an experienced journalist able to deal with a growing proportion of live material within a fast-moving programme.

The need for training
Try at the outset to get a realistic assessment of the extra talents you already have. It may be hurtful to be told that you have an inherent weakness of voice, for example, which may never be overcome, but it is better than holding out unreasonable expectations. The main reporting techniques, including writing and interviewing, can usually be acquired with proper training. Technique *can* be picked up simply 'sitting by Nellie', but Nellie may have learned in the same way, and may have developed bad habits of her own.

Section 1: Essential

(a) Writing ability

(b) Intelligence

(c) Inquisitiveness

(d) Eagerness

(e) Persistence

Section 2: Expected

(a) General interest in current events

(b) Knowledge of specialist subject

(c) Second language

Section 3: Tools of the trade

(a) Shorthand

(b) Typing/word processing

(c) Driving

Section 4: Broadcasting qualities

(a) Speech clarity

(b) Speech tone

(c) Screen 'presence'

Check your own skills
Check off your skills in the boxes provided. At the very least you should have positive answers to all of Section 1.

Wear the right clothes for the right occasion.

Dressing the Part (1)

The attention lavished by members of the viewing public and the newspaper industry on those who appear regularly on the television screen has developed into something approaching an international pastime. Such is the level of interest, gossip and comment, it has become possible to believe that discussion about almost any night's television news centres as much on what the main female presenter was wearing – and speculation as to what it might have cost – as on programme content.

Keeping the audience's attention

Dress should not be important, but it is, because an audience concentrating on a frilly blouse, a plunging neckline or a tie with a curious motif will be distracted from what is being said. And that audience, once distracted, is lost to the reporter and the programme. So it is essential that what the reporter/presenter wears is both unremarkable and appropriate for the occasion. Extrovert clothes may be acceptable for a programme aimed at a teenage or fashion-conscious audience, not for the main mid-evening news. While a safari-style suit may look right for reporting from the scene of a jungle war, it would scarcely do for conducting a formal studio interview with a leading politician. Similarly, the 'office' suit and tie is out of place in the jungle. In both cases, common sense and good manners will offend neither the interviewee nor the viewer, who in most countries is surprisingly easily offended by lapses from what he or she understands as accepted standards of behaviour.

Programme dress rules

Programmes sometimes impose their own styles of dress on their performers as part of a co-ordinated 'look' intended to create the overall tone they wish to impart to the viewer: for example, reporters and presenters on breakfast shows may be required to wear sweaters or other casual clothes to fit in with the easy chairs and coffee tables surrounding them on the set; an evening news programme may seek to create an entirely different atmosphere by putting its talent into more formal wear and an austere set; others are known to make it mandatory for on-screen performers to wear company 'uniform', and so on. At the same time, common sense dictates that a reporter arriving first at the scene of a major breaking news story should not risk missing it by taking time to change into programme-style clothes.

If the reporter does not have a firm set of 'dress-on-duty' rules to go by – and this probably applies to the majority – the one infallible guideline is simply to dress in a way which does not invite notice. Keep the eye-catching items for off-duty days.

1

2

3

4

Dress
Clothes should match the mood of the programme and assignment.
1. The reporter covering a story in the jungle looks right in a bush shirt.
2. But formal wear is more appropriate for the studio . . .
3. . . . especially when the interviewee is 'correctly' dressed.
4. The wrong choice can create embarrassment all round.

Your appearance mustn't distract the audience.

Dressing the Part (2)

There are other problems connected with wearing the right clothes for the right occasion, because the television studio imposes some disciplines of its own. The sensitive mechanism inside electronic colour cameras can be disturbed by fine stripes or check patterns, triggering a visual vibration known as 'strobing'. Pointing the camera at some colours – notably some shades of blue – creates an electronic hole through which the studio background appears. An occasional check with programme technical or production staff will help to avoid any of these embarrassments.

Accessories
The same care should be taken with accessories: shiny jewellery can reflect studio lighting and create irritating 'flare'. Long, dangling ropes of beads, bracelets and suchlike tend to have minds all of their own in the studio or on location, and are a sure way of attracting the wrong attention – especially when they sway in the wind, become entangled in the microphone lead, or fall off.

Hairstyles
Much the same approach should be taken with hairstyles. Anything unusual is almost certain to come between the reporter's words and the audience, who are equally quick to spot changes of style or colour. For males and females alike, the best is an easily manageable combination of neatness and simplicity.

Beards
Some news programmes go to extremes and simply ban their regular male performers from the screen if they have beards or moustaches, but even those who do not usually have a sensible rule: consistency. A bearded man who suddenly appears clean-shaven is going to present viewers with an identity crisis long enough to spoil his first story or two.

Cosmetics
During the early days of television, anyone appearing before the studio camera wore make-up which resembled that used by circus clowns – white faces and green or blue lipstick. The sensitivity of modern television equipment means that nature requires little embellishment for those involved in daily factual programmes. Normal, everyday cosmetics are perfectly acceptable for females. Male faces may need only a light dusting of powder to take the shine off foreheads and noses under the studio lights, and the application of a light foundation cream will mask a 'five o'clock shadow' if shaving is not possible before a programme.

Skin tones vary, of course, so it makes sense to know what makeup is most suitable personally and to keep it handily placed for use with the minimum of delay when necessary.

1

2

3

4

Some unexpected problems
1. Check patterns and some stripes cause 'strobing'.
2. Jewellery reflects in studio lighting and causes 'flare'.
3. Be consistent with hairstyle and colouring.
4. Viewers notice even subtle changes in the appearance of their favourite regular performers.

Voice Production

With the 'look' goes the 'voice' – and probably just as much controversy. Certainly in Britain, the idea of what speech is acceptable has changed over the past thirty years. Before then it was unusual to hear any regular broadcaster who did not speak with the tone and accent closely associated with the south-east of England. Since then the arrival of local radio and television has produced a wider variety of regional accents, allowing viewers to identify more comfortably with broadcasters from their own area.

The wish to communicate

Although almost any voice will improve with training, not every one will be suitable for broadcasting. The main thing for the beginner is to *want* to communicate. This means writing for speech in a way that comes across to the listener as natural. Sentences should be constructed so that proper phrasing is possible, because that in turn will aid the audience's comprehension. The second priority is to ensure that the words, once written, are delivered with a reasonable range of inflection. Some voices become monotonous very quickly, and the more nervous the speaker the higher the pitch. So although it is easier said than done, the reporter must allow his or her voice to relax to allow the full range to come through. The listener relies on the clarity of the speech as much as on the power of the pictures, and the reporter who speaks poorly is doing only half the job.

Appointments procedures for reporters often include a rigorous voice test, and those who have been found to have lisps, other speech impediments or impenetrable accents have been denied the jobs their otherwise excellent journalistic pedigree deserved. Some speech deficiencies can be cured with practice or the attention of therapists: the viewer should be spared the rest.

Pronunciation

Another essential ingredient of the voice-and-speech process is pronunciation. This is often a matter of editorial policy rather than individual taste, because the audience needs to be sure that a name or place mentioned in last night's news is in fact the same as that repeated by someone else from the same programme tonight or tomorrow. The biggest news organisations have sophisticated methods to aid this consistency. The BBC supplies its broadcasters with a daily sheet of 'difficult' names and places in the news, supplementing this with additional pages when international political conferences, the Olympics or similarly lengthy events occur. There is also a frequently updated card index in each of the main newsrooms – together with the staff to maintain it. Not every broadcaster can afford to go that far, so dictionaries on pronunciation, a good memory, and a home-made index based on experience can be made just as effective.

```
        VOICE-OVER FOR MINISTER'S VISIT

ENG AIRPORT    Several hundred demonstrators were

               waiting for the Minister's arrival.

               But police made sure they were kept at

               the far end of the airport, well away

               from the VIP reception area. Whatever

               the protesters believe, the two

               governments have publicly stated their

               intention of improving relations between

               them, and the Minister's visit is seen

               as an important first step.

CAR LEAVES     This evening the Minister is due to pay

               a courtesy call on the President, and

               the two sides get down to business

               proper at the Foreign Ministry first

               thing tomorrow morning. The Minister

               will be here for the next four days, and

               during that time is expected to see

               leaders of the main Opposition parties

               as well as senior members of the

               Government.
```

Voice production

Write as for speech, keeping sentences short. This, combined with simple, everyday language, will help make delivery seem more natural. When setting out scripts, try to remember the convention that text appears on the right, and production instructions on the left. Mark words or phrases to help with intonation.

Speech Clarity

Successful voice production also depends on body posture and proper breathing control. Consult a voice trainer or speech therapist if you can afford it: any such lessons will be an investment in your future career. They will be well worth the financial sacrifice and are probably tax-deductible anyway.

If you are left to your own devices, read some of the many books on the subject, and make use of modern technology.

Try reading your scripts into a tape recorder and be as honestly critical as possible of the results when playing them back. Don't cheat by referring to the original material. Put it aside and listen carefully, making sure you have understood every word you have said. If not, practise until it sounds right.

A second stage might be to use a home video camera to reveal other possible faults. Some readers are surprised to discover they close or screw up their eyes when faced with unfamiliar words or pronunciation.

Whatever method you decide to use, do not be afraid to experiment with 'difficult' readings. Mastery of a range of material will give you confidence, and if you detect problems seek expert advice as soon as possible.

No smoking rules

Those who use their voice professionally should smoke very little or not at all. Michael McCallion, who taught voice at the Royal Academy of Dramatic Art and whose work includes helping actors, pop singers, and politicians in many parts of the world, also believes heavy spirit drinking should be avoided (*The Voice Book*: see page 168). It is better not to drink alcohol at all before a reading performance, so when pre-programme courtesies are being extended, keep off the gin, and stick to the tonic.

Conquering stage fright

In your early days of television reporting – whether it is on location or in the studio – nerves are bound to affect your work. Symptoms include chest tightness, faster beating of the heart, and a dry throat and mouth.

It can become a vicious circle: if you seem too nervous on screen, editors may not be prepared to risk putting you on; the less you appear, the more your confidence drains; the less confidence you have, the more nervous you will become, and so on.

The answer is to offer to do anything which will diminish your fear of the microphone. Reading off-camera voice-overs and programme 'trailers' may not be the same as full-scale reporting, but they do allow the use of your voice in public performance.

Common faults in speech
Monotonous delivery
Voice trails away at end of sentence
Difficulties in saying 'r', 's', 'v', 'w'
Emphasis on wrong word
Emphasis on wrong syllable
Final consonants missing, especially the 'g' in '–ing'
Opening letter 'h' dropped

Words commonly mispronounced

amblence	instead of	ambulance
(I) arst		asked
Antartic		Antarctic
Artic		Arctic
Australiyer		Australia
confrence		conference
crear		career
drogatry		derogatory
edyucashun		education
economickle		economical
Febery/Febury		February
Guvna (Prison)		Governor
Hospitawl/Hospitorl		hospital
ishoo		issue
Janury		January
jewring		during
jool (robbery)		jewel
Krea (North or South)		Korea
lible (to flooding)		liable
manidgement (and unions)		management
nachral (environment)		natural
nooclear		nuclear
noos (good or bad)		news
pleece		police
Pryminister		Prime Minister
saterlite		satellite
Secertry (Defence/Home)		secretary
sprise (announcement)		surprise
tempracher/temprachure		temperature
thee		the
twenny		twenty
uszul		usual
vilence		violence
wevver		weather/whether
wiv		with
yesterdee		yesterday

A Friend in the Audience

Try not to think of the audience in millions or thousands. That is far too terrifying a prospect. It will help your confidence to find a more realistic model. If the 'man in the street' is too abstract a concept, aim what you do at someone you know: a friend or family member, sitting at home on their own. Forget the camera. Instead, try to imagine you are telling your story to them alone. Try to gauge their reaction to what you are saying and how you are saying it.

Be logical
Remember that whatever you do, 'your' viewer sees it only once – and not always under the best conditions and with full concentration. Research suggests that audience comprehension of television news programmes is often very poor, even within the most sophisticated societies. Viewing is frequently interrupted, and those watching are known to be easily distracted. They misunderstand and confuse even simple stories, let alone the more abstract issues in a highly complex modern world. Help them. Make your reports for the audience, not your boss or the critics. Be logical. Use clear, direct language that everyone can understand. But do not patronise or insult the intelligence of the better-educated.

Develop a rapport
The best reporters have a rapport with their audience in a way which transcends gender or race. These are the people who inform nations about matters of seriousness and importance. As such they are welcomed into every living room every evening. They seem trustworthy and honest: that is why so many are sought after to appear in commercials.

   Who are they? Walter Cronkite of CBS was regularly voted the most trusted man in America. The big names of the late 1980s crop up regularly in discussion inside and outside television journalism. The spread and speed of the global communications satellite system has added an international dimension to the work of Kate Adie, Martin Bell, Michael Buerk, Jeremy Hands, Peter Jennings, Trevor MacDonald, John Suchet and many others. Watch them closely and see what makes them special.

Learn from others
Study your peers – especially those you admire – and try to understand them. Without consciously copying, learn from their obvious strengths and apparent weaknesses. Do not be afraid of changing your style more than once until you feel comfortable with what you are doing. If necessary, ask others for their opinions. You will soon learn to identify those whose judgement you can trust.

A rapport with the audience
One of the internationally known names of the 1980s, Michael Buerk of the BBC has won awards for his reporting of events in Ethiopia and South Africa. His experience has also brought authority to the news presenter role (courtesy BBC Central Stills)

How to Write for Television

In recognising the power of television pictures it is easy to undervalue the importance of the accompanying words. Yet the need for good writing has never been greater. Audiences are being asked to understand political, social, economic and environmental issues which will fundamentally affect their lives in the closing years of the 20th century and beyond. As a television reporter you will fail if what you provide is not comprehensible to ordinary people.

Keep it simple

Despite the welcome development of news-related programmes dealing with specialist subjects, most television journalism is aimed at a general audience. Unlike newspapers, able to target readership precisely according to socio-political groupings, television has to appeal to and be understood by all, so it must neither be too intellectual nor insult the intelligence. Your main aim must be to tell your stories in language which is: • Accurate • Clear • Simple • Direct • Neutral

Write as you speak

Something strange comes over many otherwise good journalists when they write for television. Clear thoughts become cluttered and confused, simple sentences convoluted. Direct language translates into 'officialese'.

The rule is: *think before you write*. Better still: *think aloud before you write*. The less natural it sounds, the more likely it is to be wrong. When did you last hear someone in the course of normal conversation say: 'I see the government is proposing a one billion pound cash boost for the National Health Service?' You might have heard 'I see the government's going to give the National Health Service more money. It's a billion pounds.'

Be logical

- Where possible, tell stories chronologically.
- As a general rule try to make it one short sentence, one thought.
- Understand what you are writing: if you don't, no-one will.
- Don't be put off by the language of official documents. Sometimes they are written deliberately to confuse or obfuscate, but more often the writer has no feeling for words.
- Always ask yourself: what am I trying to say? Then say it.

Avoid stupidities

Mistakes are made by reporters blind to the context of their words. Unintentional double-entendres, carelessness or insensitivities creep into broadcast material. Be alive to the changes in word usage. For example, 'gay' has a modern meaning far removed from its once better-known definition of joyful or light-hearted.

48

Reporter-speak

Language should be kept clear, simple, direct and accurate. Avoid stock phrases and clichés and stupidities. The list below is merely a taster. . .

A (one-hundred-year-old vase) comes under the auctioneer's hammer. . .	going, going, gone – for good!
Ambulances rushed. . .	do they ever dawdle?
. . . biggest manhunt since. . .	. . . the last biggest manhunt
Decimate. . .	. . . means one in ten
Every available man. . .	unavailable man couldn't be there, could he?
Full-scale (inquiry/search). . .	are they ever anything less?
Fulsome praise/tribute. . .	nearly always used incorrectly. It means insincere
Flames/smoke rose fifty/a hundred feet/miles . . .	only if it's not just guesswork
Gunned down. . .	ugh!
Helping the police with their inquiries. . .	euphemism interpreted as meaning the miscreant has been caught. Not always the case.
It's being said/called/people say . . .	reporter-speak for your own opinion
Legendary figure of the decade. . .	legends aren't created that quickly
. . . (more increases) in the pipeline. . .	keep it to gas or oil
Road blocks were set up. . .	it's routine
The explosion was heard. . .	see flames/smoke
What impact has this had on the town?	question asked at the time of the Lockerbie air disaster of 1988

Reporter-speak openers

Here behind/in front of me. . .
I'm standing. . .
It happened. . .
Security was strict/tight. . .
The lights are burning late. . .

Reporter-speak closers

. . . is anyone's guess
. . . only time will tell
. . . will never be the same again
. . . too little, too late

Good Language

The drive for reporters to use direct, conversational language does not mean that sloppiness is acceptable. What is wanted is the most appropriate and accurate word. Unfortunately, many which trip off the average writer's word processor are chosen without much thought as to their meaning.

Anyone who has the temerity to offer advice to others on the use of language is asking for trouble. But it is worth the risk to point out that it does no journalist harm to refresh the memory from time to time. For those who take pride in what they do there are many excellent reference books, from the learned to the down-to-earth, offering guidelines on structure, definitions and grammar.

Slang

The line between colloquial language and slang is a thin one, easily crossed. The distinction is made all the more difficult because the word or expression frowned on yesterday becomes absorbed into normal speech patterns today, and becomes a dictionary entry tomorrow. My advice is be cautious – let the lexicographers set the pace.

Eponyms

Where would we be without (the 4th Earl of) Sandwich, (Anders) Celsius, (Captain Charles) Boycott, (André) Amp(ère) and the rest who gave their names to household words? But there is a difference between eponyms and trade names. Not every vacuum cleaner is a (William) Hoover, nor every ballpoint pen a (Laszlo) Biro. Legal actions have been fought over careless uses which have brought trade names of products into disrepute.

Clichés

There is a long list of stock phrases kept by journalists in their writing armouries. Not that they necessarily like using them – journalists make jokes against themselves about news stories composed entirely of clichés, and would much prefer to invent elegant alternatives. Those given to the occasional lapse under pressure can be forgiven: for the rest, a close scrutiny of *Roget's Thesaurus* is strongly recommended.

Acronyms

These constitute a form of jargon. Some have passed into the language as dictionary entries, NATO and the UN among them. But they need to be understood by the writer. In military parlance the acronym SAM, for example, is short for 'surface-to-air missile' – so to describe it as a 'SAM missile' is in fact saying 'surface-to-air missile missile'. Similarly, in Britain, the 'M1': in this context 'M' stands for motorway – so to describe the 'M1' as the 'M1 motorway' is saying 'motorway-1 motorway'.

Generic terms are preferable to trade names. They avoid giving free advertising, and misuse has been known to lead to legal action. Common examples appear below.

Trade names	Generic term
Airwick	air-freshener
Aladdin	oil-heater, oil-lamp
Ansafone	telephone answering machine
Ascot	gas water heater
Autocue	television script prompter
Band-aid	first aid dressing/plaster
Bic/Biro	ballpoint pen
Black and Decker	power tool
Caterpillar	tractor
Catseye	reflective road marker/stud
Cellophane	transparent wrapping
Coca-cola, Coke	cola, soft drink
Dictaphone	dictating machine
Dormobile	minibus
Elastoplast	first-aid dressing/plaster
Fibreglass	glass fibre
Formica	plastic laminate
Frigidaire	refrigerator
Gallup Poll	opinion poll
Harpic	lavatory cleaner
Hoover	vacuum cleaner
Jacuzzi	whirlpool bath
Jeep	field car
Kleenex	(paper) tissue
Land-Rover	four-wheel drive
Lego	plastic building bricks
Letraset	instant/rub-on lettering
Levi's	jeans
Li-lo	airbed
Perspex	acrylic sheet
Photostat	photocopy
Plasticine	modelling clay
Polaroid	instant picture
Portacabin	portable building
Primus	camping lamp/stove
Range-Rover	four-wheel drive
Rawlplug	wallplug
ScotchTape	sticky tape
Sellotape	sticky tape
Singer	sewing machine
Tannoy	public address (system)
Tarmac	apron (for example)
Teasmade	automatic tea-maker
Thermos	vacuum flask
Triplex	safety glass
Underseal	rubberised coating
Vynolay	vinyl flooring
Xerox	photocopy

Avoiding Unnecessary Offence

Any heightened awareness of the importance of accurate English must take account of the need to avoid sexist, racist or other language likely to cause offence.

Sexism
Words which fail to recognise the proper place of women in modern society are offensive, especially when there are neutral alternatives. Sexist language is also often inaccurate. Progress towards its elimination is being made, particularly in the United States and Western Europe, although there is still a long way to go, and resistance to some of the alternatives which the more conservative members of the older generation especially find difficult to accept. As a reporter you should make a conscious decision to use gender-free words without going so far the other way that you will alienate the rest of the audience.

Racism
In the multicultural democracies of the 1990s, the careless or unwitting use of racist language is unforgivable. It is not usually necessary to refer to someone's colour, religion or racial origins, so unless it adds materially to the understanding of the story, don't.

It is also astonishing how ignorant some journalists are about the world's main religious beliefs (including their own, if they have them). Classic errors include references to 'Jewish churches', a complete underestimation of the importance of Islam and Buddhism, and confusion about the titles of religious leaders. Most faiths have public relations officers or their equivalent: ask them to clarify for the sake of accuracy.

Ageism
The newspaper obsession with giving the ages of virtually all those they feature is fortunately not as prevalent in broadcast journalism. The test should always be whether the inclusion of someone's age will help the audience towards a better understanding of the story.

Political labels
Labels can be extremely useful. 'Right-wing' or 'far-left', for example, are shorthand indications of the views of political figures, and an attempt to put them into context. At times they can be more misleading than helpful, because those to whom the label is applied might not agree that it is an accurate reflection of where they stand in the political spectrum. Someone described as being on 'the left wing of the Labour Party' might object on the grounds that their views are left-wing only in comparison with those colleagues who have adopted what appears to them to be more 'right-wing' policies. So think carefully before using a political label which might be contentious. Or spend a few extra words getting it absolutely right.

AVOIDING UNNECESSARY OFFENCE

Be aware of the sensitivities of others. Sexist language, for example, will often be inaccurate as well. The list below is a guide to some of the alternatives. It is not meant to be complete or definitive – or cause offence itself.

Words	. . . and better words
Businessman	business people
Chairman/woman	(in the) chair, chaired by, presided over
Clergyman	cleric, clergy
Convict	inmate, prisoner
Cripples	people with disabilities
Fireman	fire-fighter
Fisherman	angler
Freshmen	freshers/first-years
Gentleman's agreement	verbal agreement
Girl	woman (unless a child)
Her/him/hers/his	their, theirs
Ladies	women
Laymen	laity, lay people
Mankind	humanity, people
Man-hours	work-hours
Man-made	artificial, hand-made, manufactured
Man-to-man	one-to-one
Manned	crewed, staffed
Manpower	staff, workers, workforce
Man-powered	human-powered
Negro	Afro-American, Afro-Caribbean, black, etc.
Newsman	journalist, reporter
Nightwatchman	caretaker, security guard
Old	elderly
One man, one vote	one person, one vote
Policeman	police officer
Spaceman	astronaut
Spokesman	official, representative
Sportsmen	sports people, contestants, competitors
Statesman	diplomat, politician, etc.
Stewardess	cabin crew/staff, flight attendant
Warder	prison officer
Workmen	workers, workforce

Aiming for Comprehension

Experimental sessions conducted under conditions in which there are no distractions prove the comprehension levels of audiences watching television news to be depressingly low.

Many viewers have great difficulty in recalling the content of programmes they have only just witnessed, are unable to remember in detail what individual stories were about, confuse the identities of personalities and mix up geographical locations.

Neither are matters helped by the professionals' own disinclination to allow for the circumstances in which their programmes are normally viewed. They forget that interruptions of all sorts impinge upon the concentration of even the most sophisticated audiences, who are probably only half-listening anyway.

Keep in touch

There is a broadcast journalist's adage which goes: 'Say what you are going to say; say it; then say what you have said.' That has become perhaps too simplistic, but it remains a useful reminder of the reporter's priority aim – to keep in touch with the audience. What you write must be easy on the ear, understandable at the first – and presumably only – hearing, with the story as a whole built up progressively in sequence.

Signposting

Unlike the reader of a newspaper, who has come to expect the Who, What, Where and When of every story to be packed into every opening sentence, the viewer is denied the luxury of a second glance. The first duty of the writer is to tune in the audience mentally by use of a 'signpost'. This device is especially useful as an introduction to a story, or as a means of indicating a change of pace, subject or idea, as it is intended to delay the most important information just long enough for the viewer to register the context.

'Signposts' do not need to consist of more than a short phrase or word or two, especially when they are used inn the body of a story. They should not be falsely contrived, but their use should be developed consciously by every writer as part of story construction technique.

Facts and figures

Don't be guilty of assault by detail. Trade and budget figures, the fluctuations of currencies, stocks and shares – statistics of any sort – are notoriously difficult to get across with real clarity. As a general rule it is easier to take in figures as round numbers, so it is far better, for example, to describe the monthly total of unemployed as being 'nearly two million' instead of 'one million, eight hundred and fifty four thousand, six hundred and twelve'. Leave the full details for any accompanying graphics.

Signposts
Signposts are words or phrases intended to prepare viewers mentally for what they are about to hear.

Good	**Not so good**
In what's thought to be the world's worst air crash, seven hundred people have been killed	Seven hundred people have been killed in what's thought to be the world's worst air crash
The World Heavyweight Champion, Mike Tyson. . .	Mike Tyson, the World Heavyweight Champion. . .
Mortgage interest rates are going up to twelve per cent	Twelve per cent mortgage interest rates are on the way

Signpost side-headings
Tonight's headlines. . .
Now the economy. . .
Next, the Middle East. . .
At home. . .
So to tomorrow's weather. . .
Now the main points of the news again . . .

Facts and figures
Stick to round numbers where possible and let the accompanying illustration take the strain.

Figures out this morning show a fall in the number of unemployed to just below the two million mark

Production of coal has gone up again. Last month miners in the area's three pits were responsible for nearly forty-six thousand tons. . .

Places
The same principle applies to places. It is easier to refer to general geographical locations and put the detail on maps.

The factory is to be built near Luton, just off the M1. . .

Rule: first the pictures, then the words.

Words and Pictures

The test of a really good television script is whether it makes sense when heard with the eyes closed. It shouldn't – quite – because what is missing is that essential pictorial dimension. So the starting point for any journalist who hopes to become a successful reporter is recognition that words are tailored to pictures, not the other way round. It follows that the only way this can be achieved is by viewing and assessing all the available material before writing the commentary. This applies every time.

Do not be content to take the lazy way out and dash off commentaries to which the pictures are then cut to match. If you do, you might just as well be writing for radio, as the result in most cases will be dreary 'wallpaper' which adds nothing to understanding and almost certainly omits shots which would tell the story more effectively. You are also short-changing yourself, your colleagues in the camera team, and the audience.

Golden rules of writing for television

- *View the pictures and listen to the sound.* While the picture editor's technical skills, advice and collaboration are essential ingredients, the journalist must be the arbiter when it comes to editorial priorities. It is impossible to judge the work you or others have done in the field unless you are present at the pre-edit stage.
- *Choose the pictures and sound most appropriate to the story you are aiming to tell.* Pay attention to any detail which might make a good script line and try to work out roughly what you might write. Don't be inhibited or hurried into agreeing to the inclusion of shots or sequences that are irrelevant, merely pretty, or do not contribute. If your story has been allocated a duration, work to it, otherwise you risk being asked to re-edit. At the same time, always be on the look-out for qualities which make your story of greater worth.
- *Leave the picture editor to edit.*
- *Shot-list the final version.* This is second in importance only to the Rule of Viewing. Shot-listing is a means of ensuring there will be an accurate match between words and pictures. The procedure consists of noting details of the length, picture and sound content of every scene in the edited story (see opposite).
- *Write the script working from the shot-list.*
- *Record the commentary.* If there is time, rehearse to make sure the words fit. If adjustment is needed, it is easier to change the script than the pictures.

Shot-listing example

Two very famous characters who are 'married' in a top-rated soap opera are also husband and wife in real life. They have just had their first child. A big crowd of fans waits to see them take baby Soapstar home from hospital, and the News assigns a reporter to provide a short scripted item marking the happy event.

At base, picture editor and reporter complete the first three stages of the six-stage editing and scripting process.

The picture editor sets the counter to zero on his cassette player. At the end of the first edit the machine is stopped so that the writer can put down on paper everything the scene contains, together with the clock time at the end of the first shot, say three seconds.

Close-up hospital entrance	3 sec

The machine is re-started and the pictures run on to the end of the next shot, which lasts four seconds. The reporter makes a note of the details and the cumulative time:

Zoom-out to general view of happy crowd in foreground	7 sec

The procedure is repeated until the end of the edited story, when the completed shot-list looks like this:

Close-up hospital entrance	3 sec
Zoom out to general view of happy crowd in foreground	7 sec
Mid-shot Mr and Mrs Soapstar appear with baby, smiling and waving as the crowd cheers	13 sec
Medium close-up Mrs Soapstar holding baby	17 sec
Long-shot smiling nurses wave from balcony	20 sec
Medium shot car arrives at hospital entrance	22 sec
Little girl is let through crowd to hand flowers to Mrs Soapstar	26 sec
Medium shot girl returns to place in the crowd	32 sec
Medium close-up Mrs Soapstar waves	37 sec
Medium shot Mr and Mrs Soapstar get into car	41 sec
Long-shot and pan, car drives off left to right	45 sec

Using the Shot-list

Try to start writing as soon as you have completed your shot-list, before the mental picture of your edited story begins to fade. Put three words – a second's worth of script – on each line of a ruled pad, or program your computer to do so. It is surprisingly easy to lose track once you have strung 30 or 40 seconds' worth of script across a page.

Do not waste time 'polishing' your prose as you go along. Complete as much of the script in rough as quickly as possible. First thoughts often turn out to be best, and in any case you may not have very much time for elegance.

It's not necessary always to start working out your commentary from the opening shot, especially if you are prone to writer's block. Select any *key scene* – in the case of our example, probably the moment, 22 seconds in, when the young fan hands her bouquet to Mrs Soapstar – and start to write around that. Once you are over the first hurdle, the rest of the script should begin to fall into place.

Common errors

- *Mistake One* is to try to cram in more words than the duration of the pictures will allow. Given the formula of three words a second, the 45 seconds of Mr and Mrs Soapstar's activities can be covered with a maximum of 135 words if they are still to make sense. More words than that and the pictures will actually run out. Let the pictures 'breathe'. The best script is often the one with the fewest words.
- *Mistake Two* is to write without taking proper notice of what the pictures contain. Instead there are detailed references to people, places or events which do not appear. It's guaranteed to irritate the viewer, who has come to expect to see whatever is being described. The same applies to sound. If it is necessary to refer to something which cannot be illustrated, do so obliquely without drawing attention to what may be missing from the coverage.
- *Mistake Three* is to produce what amounts to a series of captions explaining exactly what the audience is able to see for itself. Sentences will be too long and the style heavy, more suited to the printed page. Let the words and pictures 'touch', lightly and sensitively. Don't state the obvious or simply repeat what is happening on the screen, and vary the length of sentences to avoid sounding stilted.
- *Mistake Four* is carelessness about accuracy. Example: if you are writing about the number of cars on the road, the shot should show cars, not predominantly lorries or buses. If you are uncertain use general terms. In this case 'traffic' would cover anything from bicycles to juggernauts.

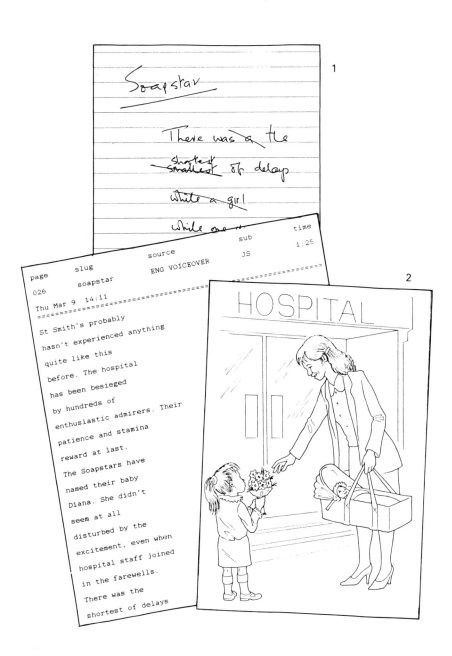

1

Soapstar

There was a the

~~shortest~~ ~~smallest~~ of delay

~~white~~ a girl

while one

time

sub

JS

1:25

page slug

source

026 soapstar

ENG VOICEOVER

Thu Mar 9 14:11

St Smith's probably
hasn't experienced anything
quite like this
before. The hospital
has been besieged
by hundreds of
enthusiastic admirers. Their
patience and stamina
reward at last.
The Soapstars have
named their baby
Diana. She didn't
seem at all
disturbed by the
excitement, even when
hospital staff joined
in the farewells.
There was the
shortest of delays

2

HOSPITAL

Picture-scripting mechanics
Write one second's worth of script – three words – to a single line on your pad
or computer terminal, double-spaced for preference (1). It's far easier to keep
track of than when stringing it across the page. Start by writing around one key
shot (2). The rest of your script should then fall easily into place.

Sample script: Baby Soapstar goes home

A typical example of the scriptwriter's art: a routine, straightforward piece of work which has no special merit but follows all the rules. Two points to note in particular: (1) the words complement the pictures, neither competing with them nor describing what the audience can see for itself; (2) the length of the sentences varies, at times straddling more than one shot.

Presenter introduction:
The latest addition to the Soapstar family made her first public appearance this morning at the ripe old age of five days.

SHOT NO.	COMMENTARY	CUMULATIVE TIME
1. Close-up hospital entrance (setting the scene)	St Smith's probably hasn't known anything quite like this. . .	0–1 sec 2 sec 3 sec
2. Zoom-out to general view of happy crowd in foreground (In reality the end of Shot 1)	. . . before. The hospital has been besieged by hundreds of enthusiastic fans. Their . . .	4 sec 5 sec 6 sec 7 sec
3. Mid-shot Mr and Mrs Soapstar appear with baby, stand smiling and waving (No script)	. . . patience and stamina rewarded at last (CHEERS) (CHEERS) The Soapstars have named their baby. . .	8 sec 9 sec 10 sec 11 sec 12 sec 13 sec
4. Medium close-up Mrs Soapstar holding baby (Not named until clearly in shot)	. . . Diana. She didn't seem at all disturbed by the excitement, even when. . .	14 sec 15 sec 16 sec 17 sec
5. Long-shot nurses smile from balcony (Telescopes action to	. . . hospital staff joined in the farewells. There was the. . .	18 sec 19 sec 20 sec

Sample script (continued)

SHOT NO.	COMMENTARY	CUMULATIVE TIME
6. Medium shot car arrives at entrance as little girl is allowed through barrier to present posy (The best moment)	. . . shortest of delays while one young admirer was let through to make her own mark on the occasion. . .	21 sec 22 sec 23 sec 24 sec 25 sec 26 sec
7. Medium shot girl returns to her place in the crowd (Commentary pause for three seconds)	. . . before it was time to go home. (SOUND ONLY) (SOUND ONLY) (SOUND ONLY)	27 sec 28 sec 29 sec 30 sec 31 sec 32 sec
8. Medium close shot Mrs Soapstar waves (The moment to add more details about her)	For Mrs Soapstar being a new mother makes no difference to her acting career. Next. . .	33 sec 34 sec 35 sec 36 sec 37 sec
9. Medium shot Mr and Mrs Soapstar get into car (Reference to him waits until they are both in shot)	. . . month she and Mr Soapstar start rehearsals for a new musical. So. . .	38 sec 39 sec 40 sec 41 sec
10. Long-shot and pan car drives off (Script ends with reference to baby who is in the car, and there are two seconds leeway before the pictures run out)	. . . far there's no part for Diana. (SOUND ONLY) (SOUND ONLY)	42 sec 43 sec 44 sec 45 sec

Introducing the Camera Crew

The special demands that 'news' makes of camera crews working along-side television reporters include the ability to think and work quickly, physical stamina, a passing understanding (at the least) of editorial values, and a willingness to accept an uncomplicated – some would say simplistic – approach to their art.

They are also conscious of being in constant local, regional, network or international competition. Crew and reporter are judged each day by results, by the pictures – or the story behind the pictures – they did or didn't get.

Staff versus freelance
The big international news services can afford to employ their own staff camera teams to cover the world. Those denied such luxury may have to share with other sections of their organisation, suffering delay and uncertain quality if news has a low priority. Other permutations include the hiring of non-staff crews contracted by the day or by the assignment, and the creation of scratch crews made up of spare production or technical staff. So although at the highest level camera crews are trained specialists, it does not always follow that the technical team knows any more than the greenest reporter about the way to tackle a story.

Camera crew numbers
In contrast to the numbers making up teams engaged on feature work, camera crews for news consist of up to three people, not counting the reporter or a producer. Cost is a factor, of course, in keeping down size, but a far more important consideration is the need for news crews to be able to travel light and work quickly under pressure, perhaps in conditions where greater numbers would be a dangerous hindrance.

Single crewing
In recent years particularly, attempts have been made to reduce the size of news crews still further by introducing better, more easily manageable equipment and combining specialisms. The growing trend towards single-person operation of camera, sound and lights is not confined to the less well-off news services, because the added benefits to be had from flexible working arrangements, speed and mobility are clearly attractive. Fears of a serious impact on employment seem to have been allayed for the most part by introducing an element of interchangeability and equip-ping each member of the team with a camera.

Despite the apparent advantages of single crewing, a cautionary note needs to be raised. One-man-bands (they were inevitably men) have always been a fact of life in remote areas, but the economies they represent have sometimes been outweighed by the indifferent quality of their product.

The shrinking size of camera equipment
The 16 mm film camera was the versatile mainstay of television news programmes for more than twenty years in peace and war. The magazine held a 400-foot roll of sound film, first mono then colour.

Electronic News Gathering. The 'Lightweight Revolution' of the mid-1970s introduced portable, three-quarter inch videotape housed in compact cassettes: instant replay replaced film processing time.

Half-inch, the format of the late 1980s. Excellent picture and sound quality is available as one- or two-piece camera/recorder units, some of them based on equipment for home use. The accent is on economy and mobility, which puts teams into the field equipped with recording and editing facilities (courtesy Key West)

Camera Crew Who's Who

The duties carried out by members of the typical news camera crew fall into two main categories – picture and sound. A third element – the provision of artificial lighting – is not always necessary. When it is, it can be supplied either by use of the limited range of equipment carried by the crew, or by another technician.

Camera

In news the person who operates the camera (US: photographer) is traditionally the senior and more experienced half of a two-person crew. Responsibility includes placing the camera in position, composing the picture and shooting the scene. Veteran camera-people are also respected for editorial understanding collected over many assignments; although the reporter is nominally in charge, if you are sensible you will always listen to advice when it is offered.

Sound

The recordist is chiefly responsible for operating the sound recorder, ensuring speech levels are balanced and choosing the right microphone for each assignment. This has become more difficult with the introduction of stereo sound. The recordist's technical expertise has also been extended to include first-line maintenance of the equipment. As a help towards promotion the recordist may also be given opportunities to use the camera under supervision. Recordists probably stand to benefit most from the move towards single or joint crewing, as the separate categories will be swept away. The recordist's technical expertise has also been extended to include first-line maintenance of the equipment.

Lights

Lighting assistants – electricians or 'sparks' – probably operate independently of the rest of the team. Their equipment consists of a portable rig of hand-held and free-standing lights powerful enough to provide illumination under which tape or film can be shot at indoor or poorly lit locations. As each new generation of camera lenses becomes more versatile and light-sensitive than the last, the number of occasions when separate lighting is needed is being reduced.

Getting there

Camera operator and sound recordist work closely as a team, often with their own transport. Increasingly their unobtrusive saloon cars are being replaced with more substantial vehicles equipped to transmit material direct from the scene. Some news organisations have gone one stage beyond, combining camera crew and reporter, picture editing and transmitting facilities into a single, self-contained mobile unit.

Camera
Composes picture,
shoots scene.
Offers advice
to reporter.

Sound
Operates recorder,
chooses microphones.
Maintains equipment
for crew.

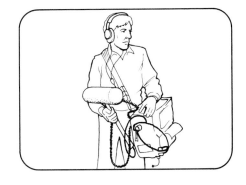

Lights
Sets up lights
at poorly lit
locations. Finds
power source.

Importance of Camera-people

Despite the important separate skills each member of the supporting technical team contributes towards the work of a reporter, those offered by one colleague stand out above the rest: whoever operates the camera comes between you, your ideas and their execution.

It is a curiosity of television journalism that it concentrates such power in the hands of a non-journalist; whatever motives are ascribed to and criticisms made of reporters, strangely little attention is paid to camera-people, who make an editorial decision every time they point the lens at one scene in preference to another. This is in complete contrast to radio or print journalism, where the technicians have a wholly non-editorial role, and where their assistance does not come into the reckoning until the reporter's work is finished.

So it is arguable whether a television reporter can ever be any better than the camera will allow. Certainly the role is a crucial one, and the early stages of your career can in large measure be made or marred by the temperament and ability of those assigned to operate the camera; you can learn a lot about your own job from the way your colleagues go about theirs.

Discuss content

Try to strike up a good relationship right from the start. Get into the habit of discussing the proposed shape and content of your item before you begin work and, particularly when you are still inexperienced, be guided by the experience, advice and ideas of others. Be trusting. You will rarely be let down: professional pride makes camera-people say 'if the reporter fails, we all fail'.

Nevertheless you are always expected to take the lead, however green you are, so the relationship can be a difficult one. At times it may be necessary to insist on following through your own ideas against what may seem to be better judgement. If and when you are proved wrong, be big enough to admit it.

Sensitivities

It is equally important not to overlook the professional sensitivities of others. For example, never attempt to 'play the director'. It's time-consuming and can seem pretentious, as television journalism does not go in for feature-film technique. Wait to be invited to look through the viewfinder when a shot is being composed. If it happens it is a privilege not to be taken for granted.

Finally, remember that the camera operator's responsibility for pictorial content includes an awareness of the need to shoot pictures with deadlines and the editing process in mind, so in hard news situations do not expect other than sharp, unfussy camera-work.

The importance of camera-people
The television reporter is part of a team, so make full use of the experience of others working with you. Camera-people who take a pride in their work are happy to pass on their expertise to young reporters, and will do their best to ensure a successful end-product. But they don't respect arrogance or over-confidence.

Camera Equipment

Camera equipment has come a long way since the days when the newsreels went to war with the 35 mm gear similar to that used in the making of feature films. First there was a switch to the lighter, more mobile 16 mm – originally regarded as amateur equipment – complete with magnetic sound track, fast chemical processing and modern editing techniques. Twenty years later, towards the end of the 1970s, came a further revolution which saw film virtually swept away altogether in favour of reusable, instantly replayable videotape. The after-shocks of that revolution are still being felt as the developments in electronics and computer technology spearhead the drive towards even smaller, lighter tape and cameras and comparable improvements in the quality of picture and sound.

Electronic news gathering
The commonly accepted term for the lightweight video equipment used in news is Electronic News Gathering (ENG), although other terminology, including Electronic Journalism (EJ) and Portable Single Camera (PSC), also exists.

ENG in any guise consists of a camera weighing a few pounds/kilograms and a portable videocassette machine on which picture and sound are recorded. Some models combine both functions in a one-piece 'camcorder' (camera-recorder).

The first widely used ENG equipment ran on three-quarter-inch (19 mm) tape, but this has begun to be superseded by Betacam, a half-inch (12.5 mm) tape system introduced by the Japanese company, Sony. The original Beta is now being replaced in its turn by Betacam-SP (Superior Performance), with which television news organisations all over the world are busily re-equipping. Although any size of tape can be transferred electronically to another, the switch to Betacam represents a huge investment for those able to make it.

Improvements have also made the half-inch VHS home video system suitable for professional use by some news services seeking economy as well as high technical standards.

The advantage of ENG
ENG's principal advantage for news work is its speed, as there is no wasteful processing time. It is also extremely versatile in other ways. The videotape cassette can be extracted and handed over for despatch and editing; the signals can be transmitted direct to base or an intermediate microwave link; they can be transmitted live and recorded at the same time. The tape is cheap and reusable, and the pictures and sound can be transferred by playing them from one cassette to another without obvious loss of quality. Material edited electronically is never actually 'cut', the original remaining intact.

68

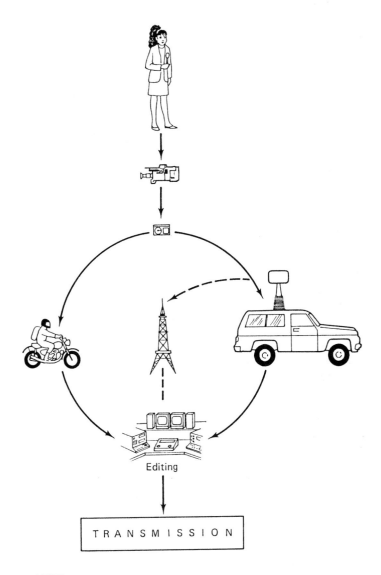

Editing

TRANSMISSION

Advantages of ENG
One-piece camcorder offers speed and flexibility. Sound and pictures can be
recorded onto tape for delivery by hand or transmitted over microwave link
direct to home base, or to an intermediate point. 'Live' transmission facilities are
also possible, if necessary via satellite.

Don't let the stick mike wave about.

Sound

One-piece camcorders come equipped with a microphone clipped to the top of the camera body. It picks up sound from the direction in which the camera is pointed. On some models the microphone can be removed from its cradle and hand-held by the reporter or another member of the team. Other ENG systems have leads plugged into the cassette recorder, allowing a variety of microphones to be attached according to location and conditions. Four main types are in use for news.

Personal microphone
This is light, inconspicuous and particularly favoured for use by reporters and subjects in interviews. It comes in at least two versions – one is attached to a cord which slips over the head, while another (also known as a lapel microphone) clips directly onto clothing. Both rest at about chest height, so helping to keep out background noise. In either case the connecting lead, which looks untidy if seen in shot, can be easily hidden from view.

Directional microphone
Sometimes known as the rifle or gun mike, it is aimed at the speaker by the recordist. Its long, thin barrel is usually covered by a metal baffle as protection against wind noise. This microphone picks up sound through a narrow angle over long distances. Its drawback is its unfortunate weapon-like shape – highly dangerous in some circumstances – and the tendency for handlers to let it creep into shot.

Stick microphone
This is the simplest in the recordist's bag. It is extremely popular for use by reporters doing stand-up pieces. Very little preparation is required, and it is adaptable for most purposes. Grasp it firmly near the head. If you are using it during an interview it should be 'favoured' gently towards the speaker and not thrust forwards aggressively.

Radio microphone
With the advantage of allowing you freedom from any cable attachment to the camera equipment, the radio mike consists of a personal-type microphone and a miniature transmitter which slips into the pocket. The device enables your voice to carry over several hundred yards/metres and, used sparingly, can be very effective.

Other microphone types
These are more likely to be used in studios than on location. Stand mikes offer high-quality sound at the expense of obtrusiveness, and boom mikes (directional microphones controlled by boom operators) can create annoying shadows.

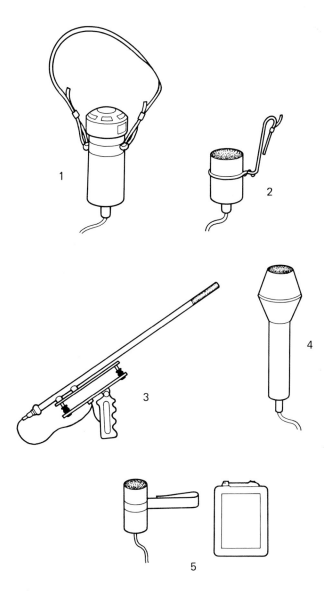

Microphone types
Personal microphones come in two types, one with a cord which slips over the head (1), and another which clips on to clothing (2). Directional microphones (3) have a weapon-like appearance. The stick microphone (4) is versatile and soon ready for use, while the radio mike (5) comes in two parts – a personal microphone and a miniature transmitter.

Stand-uppers

The stand-upper (stand-up or piece to camera) has always been con-sidered one of the mainstay techniques of television reporting, although it goes in and out of favour according to fashion. It remains a yardstick against which confidence in front of the camera is measured, and while there is nothing complicated about the technique, no reporter is likely to make serious career progress without mastering it.

The term speaks for itself. The stand-upper consists of a straightforward spoken delivery to the camera – and through it to the audience. Also:

● It establishes the reporter's presence on the spot.
● It takes little time to do.
● It offers versatility because it can be used by itself or as a single ingredient within a story.

Given a choice, some reporters prefer not to use the stand-upper at all, believing they have failed if they have to resort to their own talking head instead of what they consider should be more adequate illustration. Others are reticent because, surprisingly, they lack the technique, which depends on three things:

● An ability to compose direct, spoken language.
● A good memory.
● Fluent, confident delivery.

The emphasis on good, broadcast-style writing has already been stressed, so let us examine the other main requirements.

The right backgrounds
These are essential to all stand-uppers, which are intended to prove to the viewer that reporters are where they say they are. Pieces to camera are enhanced by relevant backgrounds, which should always be preferred to those offering only anonymity. It's worth taking time to investigate the most appropriate setting, but be sure to consult your camera crew before deciding where to place yourself. Don't allow so much to go on in the background that the viewer will not be interested in what you have to say. Noisy settings can be just as distracting. And never leave the audience wondering why a particular background has been chosen. Opening words must be sure to set the scene.

Centre-screen or to one side?
Some news organisations like their reporters to be positioned in the centre of the picture while delivering stand-uppers. They believe it adds authority. Others with an eye on the composition prefer the performer to stand to one side or the other, arguing that in this way the reporter becomes part of the scene and does not appear to be a superimposition on it. You may not be given the choice. If you are, err on the side of consistency.

Stand-uppers
Find an appropriate place from which to tell your story. A background will put your piece in context (1), but take care not to distract the audience by cluttering the screen with too much detail (2). An anonymous setting is boring and adds nothing (3). Some news organisations prefer their reporters to be positioned centre-screen (4). Others believe picture composition is enhanced by placing the reporter to one side.

Learn your script in limerick lengths.

Memory Aids

The most obvious problem you face in preparing your first stand-upper is remembering the words. For those whose nerves let them down to the extent that they are unable to memorise anything, ad-libbing is not the answer. It rarely comes across as convincing, especially if it is not fluent, and in circumstances where strict accuracy of thought and language are necessary, it can be very risky.

How to remember the words
For the beginner, the secret is to proceed cautiously and not to be over-ambitious. First, write down what you are going to say and memorise it. If you can remember a five-line limerick you can manage 30 words – the equivalent of ten seconds. When that seems easy, increase it in 15-word – five-second – stages until you have reached a comfortable, sensible limit.

Alternatives
If circumstances demand that your piece lasts for 40 seconds, and the best you can manage is 20 seconds, do not try to speak your lines in one continuous take. Seek the co-operation of the camera crew in learning and recording your words in two separate chunks. Make sure you are framed sufficiently differently in each half so the result will not look odd when the two takes are edited together. It is ugly but effective.

Another way out is to ensure that at least the opening and closing paragraphs are word-perfect, and to read the rest from a notebook or clipboard. Make sure this is in shot, or viewers will be left wondering what you are looking at.

Electronic prompting
Technology is on hand if none of these methods works. Field versions exist of the electronic prompting devices normally used in studio work (see page 120), though these tend to be reserved for scripts associated with lengthy documentaries rather than straight news.

Miniature tape recorders
A second, increasingly used aid comes in the shape of the tiny, battery-operated cassette machines used as audio-notebooks or as players of pre-recorded music tapes. First, the stand-upper script is written and recorded. The recorder is then kept out of shot while the reporter performs for the camera, listening to the replayed tape through the earpiece and repeating the words aloud. With practice this is the most effective method of improving fluency of delivery, although it is obviously important to be able to keep a sentence or so ahead of the recording and to concentrate on speaking as well as listening. The earpiece must fit snugly enough not to give the game away. And don't forget to change the recorder batteries.

Aid to memory

If you lack confidence in your ability to remember lines, a miniature tape-recorder with attached earpiece (1) will make you appear fluent under almost all circumstances. Once you have written the script (2) and recorded it, put the machine in your pocket. The earpiece is visible from the side as you speak, prompted by the replayed tape (3). Take proper care, and the camera – and the audience – sees only a confident performance (4) (Author). A less sophisticated aid is the 'idiot board' which, at its crudest, consists of a handwritten script held below or to one side of the camera.

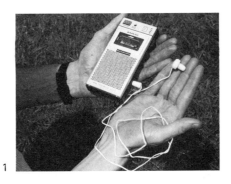

1

2

3

4

The Art of Interviewing

Interviewing is an art, to be approached with careful thought for what you aim to achieve. There is more to it than the routine, all-purpose line of questioning which scarcely varies whatever the topic – the journalistic equivalent of the sales-pitch. The best interviewers are not satisfied unless every time they appear they unearth a small nugget of truth or open the door to wider understanding.

Beginners have a tendency to think of television interviews only in terms of the lengthy, combative set-pieces conducted in studios at prime time, and are surprised to discover the existence – in addition to those for news as 'bites' or parts of packages – of a wide range of types, each calling for subtle differences in treatment.

Preparation
The first rule of interviewing has nothing to do with journalistic ethics or technique. It is: *find out who you are interviewing and why.* Don't wait until the camera is rolling and expect the interviewee to come to your rescue. Some will; others will relish the opportunity it presents. Nothing is more guaranteed to undermine your credibility with the audience and dent your confidence than an interview which gets off on the wrong foot, the subject prefacing the answer to your first question with the correction to a name or title. Embarrassment all round – at your expense.

Once you are armed with the basic details, ask yourself what you expect from the interview. Facts for the record? An opinion? Or a mixture of both? Is it to be short and incisive, or leisurely and gently probing?

The extent and depth of your research will of course vary according to the kind of interview involved. A thorough examination of background material is more likely to be necessary for a searching political interview than with the eye-witness to a robbery.

Questions
Some journalists do not prepare questions in advance, preferring to 'wing it' and let the interview run its natural course. There are very few circumstances in which this is a good idea, and even fewer practitioners who can get away with the technique. Spraying questions about as they come to mind is undisciplined and is bound to lead to confusion, omission and repetition.

But unless there is a danger of running out of questions, there is no need to write down a long list and stick to it regardless. If you are afraid of 'drying', it's worth jotting down a few to jog the memory, but it is more spontaneous to have a broad outline of the areas to be covered and to leave the detail until the interview gets under way.

The set-piece interview (1)
One of the main categories to be found either in the studio or on location, the classic single-camera set-up has the lens pointing over your shoulder at the interview subject.

Detailed rehearsal ruins spontaneity.

Interview Preparation

Most interviews benefit from spontaneity, so it is not a good idea to go over questions in detail. For the same reason avoid 'dry runs' or rehearsals with or without the camera, which risk nervous or inexperienced interviewees 'talking themselves out' before the real thing begins. But as the purpose of any interview is to extract something of value for the audience, the subject should be given a general idea of the ground to be covered and the shape the interview is intended to take.

Submitting questions
Do not readily agree to submit questions in advance unless it is the only way of securing an important or much sought-after interview, and – apart from rare and unusual circumstances – do not concede the right of veto over part or all of the finished product.

Judge on its merits a condition that an interviewee will agree to an appearance on the strict understanding that a particular subject will not be covered or a particular question not asked. It depends on how badly you want the interview. Quite often, as a well-conducted interview proceeds, it becomes possible to raise the contentious issue after all. On other occasions, if it would appear ridiculous not to ask the burning question of the hour, a refusal to answer – and the manner of that refusal – may be worthwhile in its own right. But once you have accepted conditions, stick to your word. Anything else would be unethical.

Tone
Much of the criticism made of interviewers is to do with their 'tone'. Accept that you will rarely be judged as having got it exactly right. Viewers' opinions are inevitably coloured by their own prejudices and perceptions, and it is not unusual for one half of the audience to believe, quite genuinely, that you have been too hard and aggressive and the other half – just as genuinely – that you have been too soft and tentative.

Faced with this conundrum every day, try to forget how the audience might react and seek to adopt a tone which suits the occasion. Sometimes it is necessary to pursue an interviewee who appears to be trying to avoid giving answers to legitimate questions. Regrettably that has become a tactic commonly employed by politicians and others. But there are basic courtesies to be observed, and remember that interviewees have the ultimate sanction: they can always walk away if they do not like the way they are being treated.

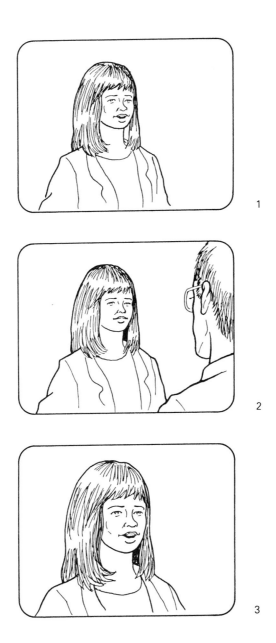

Set-piece interviews (2)
The set-piece is usually shot in medium close-up, concentrating on the interviewee (1). Rather than stop the camera, ensure any running changes to composition are carried out during your questions (2) which can then be edited out (3).

Rule: ask questions, don't make statements.

Interview Technique

The technique of interviewing for television is very different from that used by journalists who work in the medium of print. Newspaper journalists are able to conduct their interviews over the telephone or in some quiet corner accompanied by nothing more technical than a drink, pencil and notebook or miniature tape-recorder. The occasion can be formal or informal to suit, with questions asked and clarification sought in any manner which seems appropriate. Questions and answers do not have to be grammatical or follow a logical path, for once back at the keyboard the journalist can tidy up the product and make it fit any desired shape.

The television reporter's work is nothing if not public. At the very least the interview is conducted in the presence of one technician with the camera, which immediately creates an air of artificiality. And then the interviewer's technique is subjected to a scrutiny to which the newspaper journalist is never put.

Putting the questions
There is always an element of 'performance' in every interview. Be conscious of it, even though your questions may be edited out.
● Don't gabble.
● Be clear and unambiguous.
● Ask questions, do not make statements which leave the interviewee wondering whether to answer.
● Keep questions short, but not so short that they scarcely register.
● Remember that the audience is more interested in the interviewee's answers than your questions.
● Once you have asked a question, let the interviewee answer. If you have to interrupt, do so when there is a natural pause. Recordings of overlapping voices are impossible to edit.
● If an interview strays too far off the subject, bring it back on course. If necessary, stop the camera, explain to the interviewee what is going wrong, and start again.
● Avoid 'warm-up' questions. They waste time.
● Do not preface every question with deferential words or phrases which suggest timidity. Typical examples: 'May I/Could I/Do you mind if I ask...?'
● Be bold and direct – but being too brusque will be counterproductive.
● Take care not to ask questions which invite one-word answers, usually 'Yes' or 'No'. Rephrase.

Supplementaries
Some novice interviewers concentrate so much on asking their questions that they forget to listen to the answers. Always be prepared to ask supplementaries, and if the interview suddenly takes off in an unexpected, more interesting direction, follow.

80

1

2

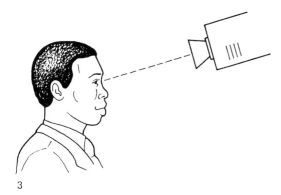

3

Interview technique

Position the subject slightly to one side, looking towards the empty side of the screen (1). 'Profile' shot has the interviewee looking out of screen and seeming to exclude the audience (2). The camera operator's view should be two to three inches (50–75 mm) above the subject's eyeline (3).

Cliché questions

Some questions are asked so frequently they have become clichés. Avoid especially:

- How do you feel (about)...?
- What of the future?
- What's your reaction to...?
- Just how serious...?
- Just what...?
- Just when...?
- Just why...?

These are just irritating.

Interview Types

Most interviews fall into one of a limited number of categories. At this stage it is important to differentiate, so what we are examining here are those conducted out on location with an ENG team. Interview types which take place in front of the studio cameras are discussed on pages 126–143.

Set-piece interviews

Set-pieces provide much of the bread-and-butter material for inclusion in reporter packages (pages 86–91). They presuppose the interviewee's willingness to participate, which means that on occasions arrangements can be made far enough in advance for the reporter to undertake some proper preparation.

This form of interview is likely to take place on the interviewee's own ground, and will tend to be used to gather opinion and interpretation rather than fact.

A typical set-piece for news-related programmes probably consists of no more than six or seven questions. Make sure the interview follows a logical pattern with a recognisable beginning, middle and end, so that afterwards it is possible to select a coherent chunk rather than edit fiercely. Less time will be spent in the cutting room and what appears on the screen won't seem 'bitty'.

Put the interview in context by setting it against a relevant background. If there's a sensible alternative to the anonymous office, use it. During the interview the camera will probably point over your shoulder at the interviewee, framed in medium close-up, and only your voice will be heard. Any necessary changes of shot and angle should take place only during the questions, which are likely to be edited out of the final version and replaced with 'cutaways' (see page 84).

Doorstepping

The term 'doorstep interview' is more or less self-explanatory. The reporter waits – sometimes literally on the doorstep of a building – for an interviewee to appear. A special target may be in mind, or it could be that anyone who is willing to talk will be pounced on and interviewed.

Questions are usually straightforward – typically connected with the outcome of official meetings or negotiations.

Doorstepping tends to be a fairly hit-or-miss method of interviewing. It is not much liked by reporters, although some useful material is often forthcoming. It is also surprising how regularly what begins as a shouted question from a few yards away ends with the person who has been 'doorstepped' agreeing to take part in a proper interview.

Doorsteppers, by their nature, demand a large measure of patience, stamina, and willingness to push through the rest of the media crowd to point a microphone at the right person.

In the melee, don't forget to take the camera crew with you.

Eye-witness (spot) interviews

Eye-witness or spot interviews seek mostly factual information, so this is where the old-fashioned journalistic ability to persuade someone to talk to the camera comes to the fore. Eye-witnesses to accidents, other disasters, and crime, provide the stuff of hard-news reporting, and such interviews are probably the easiest to conduct. There is no mystique to the technique, but do not go blundering in with questions which are insensitive or intrusive.

Vox pops

The generally accepted accuracy of opinion polls has tended to make the use of vox pops (vox populi) in television news programmes appear out-dated. They were probably never intended as anything more than a cross-section of views taken at random, but they had the merit of providing a few ordinary members of the public with a chance to give their opinion. If used at all, vox pops are more likely now to be sought on humorous subjects.

The technique relies on exactly the same question being asked of each interviewee so that answers can be edited together without the reporter popping up in between.

One point to do with picture composition: try to have each interviewee framed in the same way – medium to close-up. 'Jump' cut effects are avoided by asking contributors to look alternately camera right and camera left.

News conferences

News conferences are group interviews, held as alternatives to separate sessions, with perhaps hundreds of journalists. They usually begin with statements by one or any number of people, followed by an open question and answer session. Unless there is a prearranged order, the problem for television reporters is how to put their question when others are trying to do the same, and at times when the camera may not be in a position to roll. To make matters worse, if there is more than one interviewee, as often happens, there is no guarantee the question will be answered by the person at whom it is directed.

As an information-gathering exercise the news conference may be acceptable, but generally it is another form of 'interview' not much liked by reporters. It smacks of news-management, because if several journalists are asking questions at once, 'the platform' is likely to choose not to hear the most awkward ones. The ideal solution is to shoot some scene-setting material and seek separate interviews afterwards. If this proves impossible, take your chances along with everyone else. Make sure your recordist positions the microphone on the 'top table', preferably fixing it firmly to the public address mike. In that way you are sure of picking up all the answers clearly, and if necessary voice-over questions can be added later.

Cutaway Questions

Reporter cutaway questions (inserts or reverses) are recorded in case the picture editor needs to bridge chosen sections of an interview shot on a single camera. It is a cinematic editing device, the intention being to avoid the ugly, on-screen 'jump cut'.

For the reporter, the technique relies on an ability to repeat the original questions for the camera as naturally as in the interview, even though the interviewee is probably no longer with you. Consult your original list or replay the interview to ensure keeping to the questions as closely as possible. Some sticklers for accuracy record their interviews on personal cassette-machines and play them back before asking the cutaways. While it is probably just about acceptable to tidy up the occasional grammatical error, be careful not to cheat by putting an entirely different construction on a question.

Noddies

Serving the same purpose as the cutaway is the 'noddy' – a shot of the reporter nodding in response to the interviewee's answer. This device should be used sparingly, as a 'noddy' could give a misleading impression that you agree with what is being said. Some news organisations ban 'noddies' and cutaway questions altogether, in the belief that the viewer has a right to be aware that editing has taken place.

Both devices depend on a correct positioning of the camera. If it is wrong, the edited version will give the impression that interviewer and interviewee are looking in the same direction, not at each other.

Interview editing

In countries where a degree of press freedom exists, it is understood that television interviews are subject to editing, those for news and news-related programmes most of all.

Yet the whole subject remains an area of controversy, an ever-present source of potential conflict – not so much with those in the public eye, but with those who are unfamiliar with journalistic practice. The complaint is then usually of 'misrepresentation' or 'distortion'. Regrettably there is often no answer which will satisfy the complainant, although it should be possible to prove that you have acted fairly and in good faith.

The main thing is never to give an undertaking to include or exclude a particular answer or passage. Whatever your own good intentions, it might be impossible to keep your promise, as the decision about editing may rest with someone more senior. In all cases, before you start to interview an inexperienced person it is advisable to make it clear that you are under no obligation to use all or any of what is said.

Cutaway questions
When a single camera is used it concentrates on the interviewee (1). Shots of the reporter are taken afterwards to act as a bridge between edited sections, thus avoiding ugly 'jump-cuts on the screen'. (2) Unless care is taken in setting up these 'cutaway questions' both interviewee and interviewer will seem to be looking in the same direction, not at each other. The technique is beginning to fall out of favour for news-type programmes.

Constructing a Package (1)

The biggest test of all-round journalistic ability comes with the creation of 'packages' combining the basic reporting skills with an understanding of television production techniques.

Packages have no set shape or duration, but as the reporter's way of story-telling they must follow a clear, logical thread and sustain interest, whatever the subject.

Occasionally, especially at first, you may have an editorial help-mate to guide you through the intricacies. Mostly, you are on your own. In the past, an experienced camera team could always be counted on to make an important contribution, but with the scaling down of camera units to a size where you might be expected to operate some of the equipment as well, knowledge of production methods is an essential ingredient of your professional education.

For the purpose of this exercise, assume that the team consists of three – reporter, camera operator and recordist.

Research

As we have already seen, some research, however limited, is a prerequisite for all good television reporting. It does not have to be sophisticated, consisting at its most basic only of ensuring that you and the crew are together in the right place at the right time.

Then it is important to know what the story is about. The treatment and degree of difficulty involved clearly vary according to the subject. With proper planning, including a reasonable amount of preparation time, some information can be established before you set out; background material if it exists, names of potential interviewees on or off camera.

Planning the shape

Unless they are straightforward 'hard news' stories calling for an intuitive approach on the spot, most news packages fall within a predictable framework. Variety comes from the order, number and duration of each ingredient, so the overall shape of a package can be considered and a provisional treatment planned without prejudging editorial value.

The 'recce'

Where possible take the opportunity to conduct research on the spot. While a full-scale 'recce' is a bonus – in documentary-type work it ought to be mandatory – simple matters settled in advance will add to the speed and efficiency of the camera operation when it takes place. Journalists are indeed required to be flexible in their approach, but if 'making it up as you go along' can be avoided, so much the better.

At worst, aim to arrive on the scene a few minutes before the camera team to spy out the land, make contact with contributors, decide the location of the main interviews and note requirements for supporting shots.

Current theory suggests that longer, thoroughly researched packages may also lend themselves to pre-scripting.

Whatever the subject, the typical reporter package should be so well-constructed that the audience is unaware of the joins. Voice-over commentary should dovetail neatly into and out of interview extract; the stand-upper should pick up smoothly, verbally, visually and acoustically – a tribute to the hard work, thought and professionalism which has gone into the construction of the item.

Knowing what to shoot

Camera crews rarely turn up at the scene of a news story, leap from their cars and record everything in sight. Most news gathering is better-ordered and more organised than that. It is as bad to have too much coverage as it is too little. Someone eventually has to view it, and having to plough through an hour's video rushes to select the relevant rushes for a three-minute report is unhelpful and unnecessary. The cheapness and reusability of videotape is a constant invitation to over-shooting, but this should be resisted. Raw newsfilm in its heyday in the 1960s and early 1970s came in 400-foot rolls of 16mm, and there was much discussion about the ratio of footage shot to footage transmitted, and the cost involved.

Editorial partnership

By now it should be clear that a well-constructed report is the product of a satisfactory working relationship between reporter and camera crew. But it is necessary to be aware of the limitations of equipment and the time it takes to arrange complicated camera set-ups. Understand that technical difficulties can disrupt the best-laid plans.

Usually, with experienced and co-operative camera crews, it is enough to give a general outline of what you want, but don't hesitate to act positively and direct the work to ensure that your ideas are followed through.

Accompany the crew

Every reporter should make a habit of accompanying the camera crew as they go about their business to make detailed notes about each shot or sequence. In circumstances where this is not possible, brief your colleagues as fully as possible.

The aim is to ensure that voice-over commentary makes fullest use of the available pictures, and this cannot be achieved without knowing exactly what they contain. With the right video equipment it is possible to view recorded material on site, but writing blind to other people's descriptions invariably leads to bland and unimaginative scripts.

Constructing a Package (2)

An understanding of the rudiments of film direction is a valuable asset to any reporter. This has not always been the case. When news items were short and uncomplicated it was scarcely necessary. But now that some reports qualify almost as miniature documentaries, the need has been created for better technique. Formal training is increasing, though not necessarily fast enough, and those still waiting should aim to learn all they can working alongside their colleagues in the camera crew.

The grammar of pictures
Despite the general simplicity of its approach, news filming tries to conform to accepted pictorial grammar. Audience understanding of technique has been stretched over the years by what has appeared on the big and small screen, but the conventions should not be broken unless they further enhance understanding.

In particular, do not expect to tell your story effectively through an assemblage of single, unrelated shots. Always think in sequences leading the viewer progressively towards the action: long shot, mid-shot, close-shot.

Picture composition
Few professional camera crews will like it if you insist on looking through the viewfinder before every shot. But that should not stop your journalistic eye being kept open for good backgrounds which help tell the story, or for errors in picture composition which might have been overlooked in the haste of news gathering. Try not to let interviewees appear to sprout trees, lamp-posts or other objects from their head as they speak. Look out for spectators creeping into shot or other background goings-on while the crew are absorbed in their work.

Be aware of what is written on walls over interviewees' shoulders or behind you during a stand-upper. It could be seriously offensive or inappropriate. Don't be tempted to take risks because it's in a foreign language. Someone will understand it, even if you don't. The same goes for street signs and advertisements which could distract the viewer during your report. The safe rule is: if in doubt – find another wall.

Sound
Television is two-dimensional. With the picture goes the sound. 'Natural' sound – 'effects' in this context – is often under-used by reporters who scarcely pause for breath, preferring to fill every available second with their own voice or those of interviewees.

Listen for any opportunity to make use of the natural sounds of life. They will give your work an extra quality. Some stories are simply better told by limiting the talk and letting the sound speak for itself.

Basic camera shots
Think in picture sequences, not unrelated single shots. Long-shot (1) shows the whole of a human figure; medium shot (2) shows from the waist up; medium close-up (3) shows from the chest up; close-up (4) shows head and shoulders.

Package example

STORY: the installation of a new computer system aimed at easing traffic flow in a particularly busy part of Britain.

WORKING TITLE: COMPUTER TRAFFIC.

PROPOSED DURATION: 3 min 30 sec.

OUTLINE TREATMENT: find out the reason for the project, see those at work on it and ask for their opinion of its value; contrast the beauty and tranquillity of the surroundings with the subject – traffic noise and congestion.

INGREDIENTS: shots of traffic (recent archive material if necessary); computer being installed; monitoring equipment; building and grounds; interviews with project leader; piece to camera; electronic graphics, voice-over commentary.

INTRODUCTION: by Presenter in studio, with map to show location.

ORDER OF CONTENTS:

1. Voice-over commentary to accompany recent archive pictures of traffic congestion in area (planned duration 15 sec).
2. Piece-to-camera (stand-upper) in grounds explaining how a former stately home has become a centre for the planning of road-building and traffic control (planned duration 20 sec).
3. Voice-over commentary to cover exteriors of building (planned duration 25 sec).
4. Interview (one answer) with project leader (planned duration 30 sec).
5. Voice-over commentary to show other staff at work collating information (planned duration 20 sec).
6. Natural sound as computer operators monitor traffic flow on video screens (planned duration 25 sec).
7. Voice-over commentary showing reverse angle of computer operation (planned duration 10 sec).
8. Second part of interview with project leader (planned duration 30 sec).
9. Summarising voice-over commentary showing restored part of building (planned duration 15 sec).
10. Final piece-to-camera on bridge overlooking traffic (planned duration 25 sec).

SEQUENCE	DURATION	CUMULATIVE	COMMENTARY
1	12 sec	12 sec	The planners say no-one could have possibly forecast the growth in traffic volume over the past few years. But they agree the time has now come to adopt a new approach to road-building.
2	21 sec	33 sec	Here in the grounds of a nine-hundred-year old estate less than two miles from one of Britain's busiest motorways, the roads of the future are being planned. The government has invested more than fifteen million pounds in a computer which will calculate future trends from current traffic flow. The hope is that traffic jams will become things of the past.
3	25 sec	58 sec	In the time of the Norman Conquest The Lodge belonged to a local baron who hunted boar across its extensive grounds. Probably the only sounds were those of laughter and merriment as the lords and ladies of the house feasted on chunks of roasted boar meat in the shade of the splendid oak which still dominates the front lawn. The irony isn't lost on John Smith, who's in charge of the project.
4	30 sec	1 min 28 sec	'One thing we simply have to get right. . .'
5	20 sec	1 min 48 sec	Installation work on the computer is still continuing, and the project proper won't begin until test programs have been run. But there are signs that the experts will have no lack of information on which to base their future calculations. Traffic volume has already increased by almost one per cent in the few weeks since they have been here.
6	25 sec	2 min 13 sec	'I think we should have camera four moved to give a better view of that bridge, Brian. What do you think . . .?'
7	10 sec	2 min 23 sec	But what guarantee is there that all the expense and effort going into this new project will result in forecasting which will be any more accurate than in the past?
8	30 sec	2 min 53 sec	'Well, of course there can be no guarantee. What I can say is. . .'
9	17 sec	3 min 10 sec	On the evidence of the splendour in which he lived, it's not hard to feel envious of the Baron. Nor of his successors who strive for a sensible solution to a problem of society's own making. No-one will begrudge them their comfortable life-style if they find it.
10	30 sec	3 min 40 sec	The sceptical motorist down in these traffic jams is unlikely to be convinced, however much money is poured into projects like this one. No-one pretends traffic forecasting is easy: the price of oil, the drive towards a pollution-free atmosphere and the volatile Middle East all add to the uncertainty and have an influence on the number of cars on our road. What I do believe is that hunting wild boar from the saddle couldn't have been much more tiring than driving home from the office along the crowded M180.

91

Editing the Pictures

Responsibility for editing news material is usually given to trained picture editors, but here, as in other areas of television, changing working practices and the advance of technology are leading towards the development of combination skills.

In organisations with no tradition of sealing talent into watertight compartments it is possible to find camera operators, sound recordists and others who double as picture editors. Reporters, too, are encouraged to learn editing techniques as part of their all-round knowledge.

Videotape editing

The revolution which heralded the introduction of ENG in the late 1970s also ended the era of the specialist film editor. Today's raw material for news is dominated by tape – usually three-quarter or half-inch – which is never actually 'cut'. Instead the shots chosen from the camera rushes are played from one cassette machine and recorded onto another, in sequence, until a whole report is built up. If a mistake is made, and a shot is too long, too short, or does not fit aesthetically – and above all, journalistically – the process can be repeated without harming the original material.

An additional aid is time-coding, which appears as digital clock time on the picture during editing, allowing very accurate measurement of shot duration. With some systems only clock times need to be fed into a computer, and editing takes place automatically without further human intervention. There is no rule which says the programmer has to be a trained picture editor and not a journalist.

Editing supervision

As things stand at present, a considerable amount of editing is still done by experts. The pattern in many organisations is for editorial supervision of picture editing to be carried out by producers, assistant producers or subeditors (associate producers) on the grounds that those who have been closely involved in the gathering of news are not the best placed to judge its value. Elsewhere, it is precisely this involvement which is highly valued, and the job of the reporter is to return to base with the material and supervise the editing at first hand. That said, there is often no-one else to do it anyway.

As with camera crews, mutual trust and respect has to be built up with picture editors if the outcome is to be a satisfactory reflection of separate skills. It is here that detailed knowledge of your own material and its intended usage is of paramount importance. Disagreements about the value or success of the camera team's efforts should be settled amicably, but again overall responsibility for the final version is yours.

92

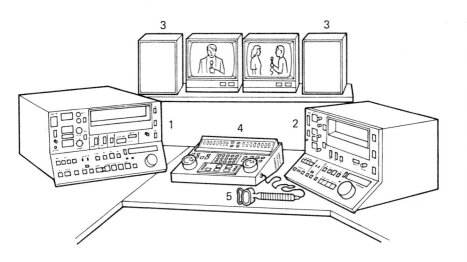

Picture editing
Editing suites for picture editing are all-electronic. The story is built up by selecting raw material from the camera – the 'rushes' – and playing it from one cassette machine (1) and recording it on another (2) in sequence. The sound is played back through linked loudspeakers (3), and a fader box (4) controls sound volume and tracks. Commentary can be recorded using a lip microphone (5).

Always view the pictures if you can.

What to Keep In, What to Leave Out

A new reporter faced for the first time with extracting two or three minutes of newsworthy material from a miniature mountain of videotape rushes will inevitably find it a daunting task. What to keep in, what to take out? And all the time the picture editor hovers, pointedly looking at the clock ticking towards your deadline.

Viewing the rushes
As a first step, view the rushes. If time is against a full viewing and there is more than one cassette, use the notes you made at the scene as a short cut to where the most important sequences are: as a matter of routine the cassettes should have been identified in order of use.

View as much of the material as you can, preferably all the way through, and try to get an overall impression. Do not allow yourself to be hurried. If you need to re-assess a shot or sequence, ask the picture editor to replay it. Compare takes and re-takes to see what worked, what did not, and why. If you are unsure, ask. Check shot details against original notes. Resolve to be more accurate next time if they do not match.

If you cannot afford the luxury of a second viewing, you will have to make a provisional shot selection as you go. Keep a record of time-code clock times and durations and try to be explicit about what you want. Ambiguity could lead to delay and time-consuming editing at a later, more inconvenient stage. Be critical of your own efforts, but false modesty is out of place.

Building up the story
Once the rushes have been viewed, the picture editor will expect your decision about the order and duration of every shot. Do not simply hand over a scrap of paper with clock times signifying edit points. That will be helpful if you have to leave to carry out other duties, but the aim should be to sit with the picture editor until you are satisfied that your ideas about construction and continuity are understood.

Interview extracts (sound bites)
There can be no firm rule about interview extracts. All news organisations have their own based on programme style. In general the more 'tabloid' or faster-paced, the shorter the interview snippet will be. So the best guidelines probably cannot go beyond three general suggestions:
- Avoid editing sound-bites so tightly that they seem unnatural.
- Make them long enough to register with the audience.
- Use interview extracts to get across interpretation or opinion while you concentrate on the facts.

Building up the story
Take care to ensure the edited story reflects all your fieldwork. View the rushes with the picture editor (1), checking duration of shots and sequences against the digital time code on the picture (2).

A poor intro can ruin the best package.

Your Place in the Programme

Some news organisations take remarkably little interest in the later stages of assignments they ask you to cover. No supervision or advice is offered, and you are left to make your own judgement about content and duration. The only support you may get is from colleagues willing to spare a few moments from their own duties to share your problems, in the knowledge that you will reciprocate when the time comes.

Comment, if any, from your superiors is reserved until after what you've done has been aired, and then it tends to be critical rather than complimentary. Unless you make a point of asking directly, the only way you may discover you are doing your job well is because no-one says you are doing it badly.

This is not necessarily a deliberate policy. In fact it is almost a compliment to be trusted to make decisions by yourself. Often the reason is pressure on time and lack of staff. Programme editors simply have too many things to do in the few hours leading to daily transmission, and previewing your three-minute item is one they can do without.

Writing the introduction

Where your news organisation doesn't run to the luxury of separate producers or newswriters, another of your responsibilities as a reporter may be to write an introduction to your own completed package. At the least you may be expected to provide a few ideas in note form.

Either way, the introductory words must be constructed in a way which keeps the audience interested enough to stay tuned in to the report about to follow. Give them as much thought as the rest of your work. Include graphics where they help. Introductions should be complementary and not include facts or phrases immediately repeated in the first paragraph of your report.

One sure way of avoiding this trap is to write a full introduction of, say, three sentences, discard the first two for the presenter to use as the introduction and begin your commentary proper with the third sentence. It works most effectively.

'Musical' news

Finally, an admission of personal prejudice against the use of background music in news items – it is often an easy substitute for natural sound effects, voice-over commentary, or an accompaniment to 'pretty' pictures. All this does is expose the reporter's lack of skill and imagination in finding the right words or natural sound.

Music, unless strictly relevant, should be left where it belongs, in the archives with the cinema newsreels.

```
===================================================================
```

```
John

cam 1 close-up _____/A plan to free Britain's motorists

                                   from traffic jams on the roads of

                                   the future has begun to take shape.

                                   The work is being carried out by

                                   the team in charge of a new

                                   computer system which is being

                                   installed in


Map _____/a former stately home in Berkshire

                                   not far from the M-180 link road.

                                   John Johnson has been finding out

                                   the details.
```

Fitting in to the programme

Introductions should complement the report the viewer is about to see. The
'Computer Traffic' package is preceded by a short script (1) to be read by the
presenter, and electronic graphics (2) to add interest (courtesy Quantel)

Leave time for things to go wrong.

On the Road

In some circumstances you will be surprised to find that it takes longer to plan returning your material to base than it does to gather it in the first place. Even in Europe and the United States, where communications are generally excellent, reporters and their camera crews often face frustration over basic mistakes or accidents which result in delay and missed deadlines.

At your own pace
Wherever possible always allow yourself enough time to do the job as you would wish it to be done. Only you know how long it takes to learn a piece-to-camera or write a commentary. Don't let the approach of hunger, tiredness or fear of offending the camera crew persuade you into a rush job or the acceptance of a performance you suspect is not up to your usual standard. Lunch can wait – the story can't.

If you are working with an inexperienced camera team or one of whom you have little previous knowledge, check the arrangements they have made for getting your material back. Fast work isn't always complemented by good organisation. In the end it is your judgement which will be questioned, no-one else's.

The hazards of going live
The flexibility of ENG, with its capacity to provide live pictures from location, has put extra pressure on reporters who might reasonably expect to spend the bulk of their time on package-making assignments.

When you are asked to 'go live' you will be linked with your programme in some way, however tenuously, and it is the responsibility of the production team at the other end to keep you informed and give the cue to begin. But don't rely entirely on other people. A few simple precautions won't go amiss. Try to get an accurate indication of when you are expected to perform – and be ready well in advance. Don't go wandering off in search of the latest information and risk not being back in time. You will seem very foolish if the studio introduction is followed by the anticlimax of a confused or empty picture that you had arranged to fill.

Coping with spectators
If possible, do your work where you will not be interrupted. The curiosity of crowds is always aroused by the onset of television activity, and you can always expect spectators to gather. If you think this may create problems, make arrangements with officials or colleagues to ensure that there is no disruption while your report is being transmitted.

Sometimes the only solution is positively to seek out the noisiest bystanders and give them the responsibility of keeping the rest quiet!

The hazards of going live
It can be extremely distracting to have spectators watching you report live. At least the crowd on this occasion was not hostile (courtesy BBC Central Stills)

Few events command genuine interest world-wide.

Covering the World

Although some issues assume a truly international dimension – world peace, oil, economic crises, disasters on the scale of Chernobyl, the Armenian earthquake and the Ethiopian famine – television journalists are interested primarily in those foreign events which have some direct bearing on the lives of the audiences they serve.

So the value of an item of news can be ranked as much according to its political, geographical or historical context as by the event itself.

Sources

Despite the often-criticised parochialism of television news, coverage of foreign issues does remain an important ingredient. For the big, internationally minded services whose audiences have come to expect same-day coverage of every important happening, it is also usually by far the most expensive part of their news-gathering operations, and every unexpected foreign story of real significance adds another strain to budgets which are frequently already over-stretched.

Television receives foreign news from several main sources:

● Local news services offer coverage of their own domestic events to the international news exchanges, which swap material between member countries over semi-permanent circuits several times a day.

● International wire services or news picture agencies have resident correspondents stationed in or close to most important international centres, and provide a large proportion of the raw material.

● Freelance journalists make their living from serving several outlets, although they may also be paid retainers by their best customers as a means of ensuring that they provide a minimum service.

● Stringers, who owe their first loyalties to the organisations which employ them, are also able to provide material to others on an irregular basis. Both these categories contain people who may not be full-time journalistic practitioners.

● Resident correspondents (see page 102) are based in countries from which the flow of important news is considered regular enough to justify the expense of having staff journalists permanently assigned.

● Foreign bureaux consist of several correspondents and ancillary staff established in particularly important centres where the presence of only a single correspondent would not be sufficient.

● The 'fire brigade' is made up of general reporters who are sent out from home base to cover specific stories, or to back up freelances, stringers or correspondents (see page 104).

● Other methods of gathering foreign material include the systematic monitoring of foreign broadcasts, often the first accurate source of 'official' news.

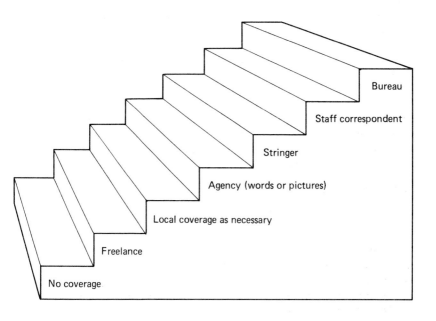

Bureau

Staff correspondent

Stringer

Agency (words or pictures)

Local coverage as necessary

Freelance

No coverage

Steps to world news coverage
News organisations grade their overseas representation according to the importance they place on an area. But foreign coverage is approximately three times as expensive as 'home' news, so, at the highest level, sharing bureaux and facilities with broadcasters from other countries' services can make economic and journalistic sense.

The Foreign Correspondent

Comprehensive news coverage of another country is best achieved by basing a staff journalist – a foreign correspondent – on the spot. The job is usually considered the most glamorous of all reporting assignments. Living in another country as the representative of an overseas news organisation carries with it social as well as professional prestige, and a correspondent who spends some time abroad builds up contacts and sources which ensure that a steady flow of news big and small is sent home.

In countries with dictatorships or totalitarian political regimes, resident correspondents of foreign news organisations are barely tolerated rather than welcomed. Restrictions are placed on their movements and what they can report, and transgressions are met with official warnings, expulsion, imprisonment or worse.

Choosing a base
In days of financial stringency, few television organisations can afford the luxury of having more than a handful of their journalists permanently off base abroad unless they are cost-effective. The areas singled out for this special treatment have to offer a proven or potentially high volume of newsworthy material, and they also have to offer efficient transport and other communications links. London, Washington, Tokyo, Moscow and Paris probably head the list of international capitals in which any news organisation of repute would always wish to be properly represented, but other centres go in and out of fashion according to their political and economic fortunes, and are kept under constant review.

Correspondent costs
The cost of keeping a correspondent anywhere does not end with his or her salary and professional needs. There are personal arrangements to be made for accommodation, transport, perhaps education for the children, and a hundred and one other things which make up a reasonable standard of living. Some correspondents have several countries or whole continents to cover by themselves, and may be expected to leave base temporarily for any part of their 'patch' where a story breaks.

The danger of 'going native'
Even the most respected resident foreign correspondents may have no more than a two- or three-year tenure in the same country, because it is considered that the knowledge and expertise they gain may be outweighed by the danger of 'going native'. For some, it becomes difficult to remain objective about a social and political scene with which they become too familiar and sympathetic, and it is better for them to move on to another country and start afresh.

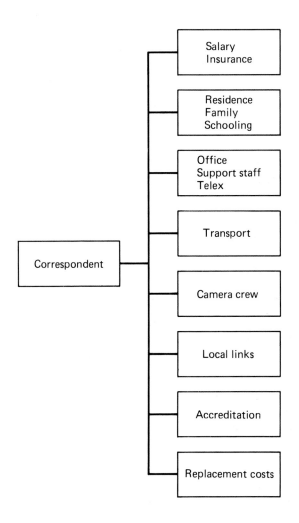

Foreign correspondent costs
Keeping a staff correspondent on permanent assignment abroad is the most expensive method of covering foreign news. Personal and associated family costs, office accommodation and staffing, and replacement of the correspondent during holiday periods all have to be taken into account.

Enter the Fire Brigade

Inevitably, the number of important foreign stories a good news organisation needs to cover each year includes many in areas not served by a
resident correspondent. And while a proportion of these will be reported
quite adequately by freelances, stringers or the agencies (see page 100),
the rest will probably demand the distinctive approach which can be
offered only by a staff journalist. This need is met by despatching one
from elsewhere, often home base. So – enter a member of the 'fire
brigade', with orders to provide comprehensive coverage, usually within
hours of arrival.

Overcoming the first barriers

Working abroad on the shortest assignment can prove a journalistic
nightmare for the inexperienced or unwary. Operating in an open society
full of helpful people is no more a guarantee of success than operating in
one where the democratic process is not developed and foreign reporters
are met with suspicion.

Any newcomer to another country is at a disadvantage, and unfamiliar
environment, language, customs and living conditions are likely to affect
the journalist just as much as anyone else, presenting barriers to be
overcome before professional considerations can be brought to bear.

Inoculations and passports

Preparation for foreign assignments should be undertaken with even
more care than for domestic ones. Those who expect to be sent abroad at
short notice should keep routinely up to date with inoculation against a
range of diseases; some countries refuse entry to people without medical
certificates proving they are not carriers of infection.

Ensure that passports and visas are valid for long enough to cover
outward and return travel. Be alert to the political sensitivities of immi-
gration officials who are on the lookout for the undesirable whose
passport bears evidence of visits to countries which their nation boycotts
or does not recognise. It pays to be especially cautious in Africa and the
Middle East, and experienced, prudent travellers equip themselves with
two passports to avoid the embarrassment – or worse – of the mark of a
tell-tale rubber stamp.

Journalists with dual nationality can also come into their own at times
when it could be a definite drawback to be the holder of a particular
passport. In 1982, when the UK and Argentina were briefly in conflict over
the sovereignty of the Falkland Islands, a surprising number of journalists
who proudly regarded themselves as British suddenly discovered long-
lost great-grandmothers in Dublin or Cork and were happily admitted to
Buenos Aires bearing Irish passports.

Typewriter
Short-wave radio and batteries
Tape recorder and batteries
Sensible clothes and shoes
Hat
Sewing kit
Shoe cleaning materials
Comb, shampoo etc.
Toothbrush etc.
Makeup/shaving gear
Other personal items such as
    Spare spectacles/contact lenses, cleaner etc.
Tummy pills
Salt pills
Water purification tablets
Foot powder
Sunburn cream
Two passports

Fire-fighting equipment
Basic equipment for a reporter on a fire-brigade assignment could include all or any of the above, depending on circumstances. Portable telephones are becoming essential accessories, and typewriters are now giving way to lap-top computers.

On Foreign Soil

Operating abroad has in many ways become much easier since the introduction of ENG. Previously, a fire brigader covering a story in another country was invariably dependent on the goodwill of the local television station for the processing of film and arrangements for its transmission by landline, microwave or satellite link as an alternative to freighting it home undeveloped and uncut. Delay and frustration were commonplace, especially at times of big stories, when it seemed that half the world's camera teams were simultaneously demanding facilities from a television station barely equipped to cope with its own programme commitments.

The independent news team
Nowadays the team assigned to a big foreign story will often include a picture editor who travels complete with a mobile editing pack so that the item can be put together on the spot. This is the ideal solution journalistically, but it remains an option open only to those organisations able to afford the cost of flying an entire team and equipment thousands of miles from base.

Setting up
An experienced picture editor can turn virtually any small room into an editing suite within an hour to provide a base for the whole operation. With careful rearrangement of curtains and furniture a hotel room can also double as a simple studio by using the team's camera. All this helps to reduce the pressure on the reporter, who can concentrate on getting the story instead of worrying whether the promised co-operation of another television organisation will be forthcoming and effective.

Unless the team is also carrying its own satellite communications dish or Feedpack – a mobile standards converter through which it is possible to transmit pictures back to base – it will still be necessary to co-operate with the local television station to have the edited material fed home.

Doing your homework
Never take anything for granted when working abroad. The simplest and most obvious matters can bring disaster if overlooked. Make allowance for the difference in time zones between one country and another: remember that a story shot on, say, the PAL 625-line television standard is incompatible with NTSC 525 lines; and that it is no good embarking blindly on a five-minute 'epic' when the assignments desk at home wants and expects a maximum of one and a half.

Camera teams are known to have missed deadlines by confusing local and 'home' times; arrived at a friendly foreign television station with important material on the wrong standard for transmission; and put all their efforts into a lengthy item intended for a programme reduced to a weekend summary.

106

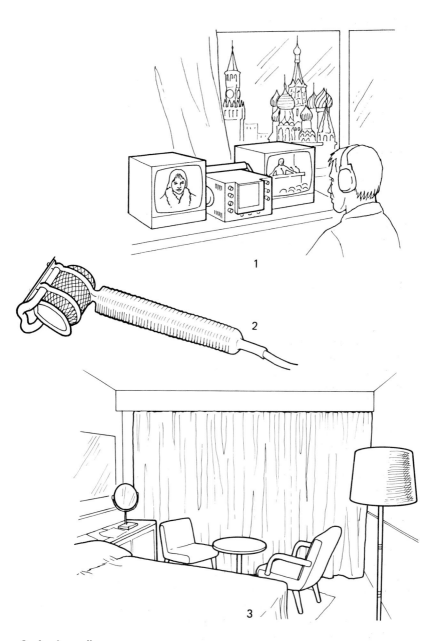

On foreign soil
Given a little effort, the average hotel room can be turned into a passable imitation of an editing suite (1). Closing the curtains will keep down noise. The picture editor will use headphones instead of loudspeakers and you can record your commentary direct onto the sound track using a 'lip mike' (2). Furniture can be rearranged to create a small 'studio effect' for interviews (3) using the ENG camera.

107

Communications Satellites

Television reporting may have undergone a revolution since videotape replaced film as the raw material of news gathering: without the communications satellite to speed the material on its way that revolution could not have been complete.

Journalists have made use of satellite technology since 1962, when Telstar was launched from Florida. The formation of the International Telecommunications Satellite Organisation (Intelsat) followed two years later, providing the impetus for a system which links continents to ensure same-day news coverage from virtually anywhere in the world.

The first satellite in the Intelsat series was known as Early Bird, and 'birding' has become the accepted term for the entire process of transmitting news by satellite. Intelsat, with its headquarters in Washington DC, has a membership in excess of one hundred countries, most of which are represented by their national telecommunications organisations.

How satellites work

Communications satellites are launched into orbit 22,300 miles above earth, at which point they appear to be stationary. In this way global coverage could be achieved, in effect, with one satellite over each of the Atlantic, Pacific and Indian oceans. In fact there are several satellites over each region to cope with the increased traffic – particularly over the busy Atlantic region – and to cover breakdown.

Sound and pictures are sent across continents from one earth station to another via the satellite, which amplifies the signals as well as transmitting them. Television makes only some use of the available communications capacity: the latest generation of Intelsat satellites has a capacity to carry more than 30,000 simultaneous telephone conversations as well as three television channels.

In the late 1980s television began moves towards the era of DBS (Direct Broadcasting by Satellite), a method by which signals are directed to individual homes rather than nationally owned ground stations. The satellites have been built for operation by individual governments or commercial consortia.

Satellite news gathering

Such is the need for reliable communications that a number of the richer news organisations have found it worthwhile to invest in their own mobile earth stations. These can be packed into lorries or aircraft to meet the demands of big stories in remote areas, providing instant access to pictures. Self-contained satellite news gathering teams consisting of reporter, camera crew and picture editor, supported by technical staff and facilities, have added an extra flexibility to news gathering. The capital investment is offset partly by bypassing the commercial ground stations in the transmission chain.

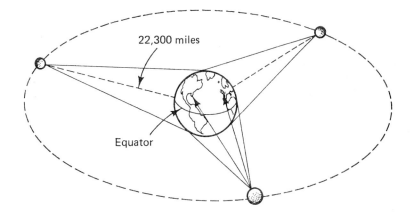

22,300 miles

Equator

The global satellite system
Television signals are beamed 22 300 miles into space to satellites orbiting the earth. There they are received, amplified and transmitted to ground stations on the other side of the globe. Intelsat, the International Television Satellite Organisation, operates satellites over the Atlantic, Indian and Pacific Ocean regions, effectively covering the world.

Staying Alive

Journalism can be a dangerous business. There are always those who wish to keep their activities hidden and are prepared to go to extraordinary lengths to prevent any attempt at uncovering them. They are not always swayed by arguments about truth, justification, or the national or public interest.

Some regimes get over this problem by simply refusing to open their borders to anyone they consider 'unsympathetic'. Short of illegal entry or posing as a tourist, no reporter can do much about that, and then the consequences of exposure are obvious. Other countries allow in foreign journalists, but impose strict censorship and other conditions which may or may not make it worthwhile being there at all.

It is in these countries, especially, where it is important to be aware that an interviewee encouraged to be outspoken on camera might be 'visited' by the authorities once you are safely back home.

A third category allows journalists in to report what they want – but at their own risk. Parts of Latin America, Africa and the Middle East have proved particularly dangerous in recent years, with wars, civil unrest or general lawlessness making reporting extremely difficult. Death, injury, abduction or imprisonment have befallen hundreds.

The vulnerability of television

Because they do not operate alone, television journalists are conspicuous and therefore especially vulnerable in hostile conditions. The presence of a camera team at a potential trouble-spot is often sufficient to attract unwelcome attention. Depending on the sophistication of those seeking to be disruptive, harassment may range from the minor (a hand over the camera lens or cutting the lead between cameraman and sound operator) to the serious (smashing the equipment) to the very serious (physical attacks on the crew).

Camera teams also find themselves arrested and bundled off for no apparent reason, and although apologies and release may follow fairly swiftly, the damage – removal from the scene – will have been done.

The alternative to arrest is often a demand to hand over such material as has been shot. When faced with this position in democratic countries, the response to police should be to insist that the proper legal process is followed. This is not, however, an approach to be encouraged when the request is made at gunpoint.

Protection for journalists

The International Press Institute has been concerned with the protection of journalists since it was established in 1951, and other professional bodies have also made attempts to present a united front against the harassment and maltreatment of journalists doing their job. Many news organisations issue their own guidelines to staff in dangerous areas.

Red Cross lifeline
Since 1985 the Press Division of the International Committee of the Red Cross in Geneva has operated a 24-hour lifeline for journalists captured, arrested or held in detention while on professional assignment. The line is available for use by the families, editors and professional organisations of journalists in trouble. Address: 17, avenue de la Paix, CH-1202, Geneva, Switzerland. Telephone: (area code 22) 34 60 01.

The Journalist's Survival Code

- You are more important than the story. No story is worth your life.
- If you are threatened, get out as fast as you can.
- If authorities can't guarantee your safety, leave the country.
- Never carry a gun or other weapon.
- Never point your finger; it can be mistaken for a gun.
- Know the country, the region and the people involved.
- Know the language at least well enough to identify yourself and to talk to local residents.
- Always carry complete identification papers.
- If you are in an unfamiliar area, travel with other journalists who know it well.
- Know all your journalistic colleagues in dangerous situations. Strangers may not be what they seem.
- Outcries against abuse provide protection. Resist abuse by authorities and always protest (about) such abuse of yourself and other professionals. But don't become abusive yourself.
- Avoid unknown risks. Vague promises of a story often come from persons who can't guarantee your safety.
- Stories in remote locations far from authority and medical assistance present added risk.
- Do not masquerade as other than what you are. It raises suspicions and creates risks for other professionals.
- Under no circumstances accept compensation from or do work for a non-journalistic or government information-gathering intelligence agency.
- A professional must maintain a standard of truth despite risks and dangers. Some stories are worth more risk than others.
- Avoid bias for one side or another. Do not cross the line between journalist and active participant.
- Weigh what you know about the risks against the possible benefits of a story. Often, a story is just as good if covered from a distance.
- Distinguish between risk and present danger. Avoid obvious danger and don't take undue risks. Often discussing this with friends and colleagues can help.

111

- Avoid reporting from both sides of a conflict if possible. Crossing from one side to the other is always dangerous.
- Always carry a white flag.
- Always use extreme care in selecting competent locals as drivers, guides, etc. Their presence of mind is a protection.
- Mark your car clearly as 'Press' in the local language.
- Use two cars where practical in case one breaks down.
- Never wash your car. Unwanted tampering can be detected easier on a dirty car.
- Talk to local residents as much as possible and listen to their advice.
- Dress appropriately. This will vary. Sometimes you will want to blend into a crowd; at other times you may want obviously not to be one of the group.
- Never wear olive green or anything that makes you look like a soldier.
- Let your desk or editors know where you are at all times, where you are going and when you expect to return.
- Let your colleagues at the hotel know the same thing.
- When confronted by hostile persons, identify yourself in their language and attempt to convey ideas about what you are doing.
- If guerrillas at roadblocks ask you for a 'war tax', give something. It shouldn't be much, but it can avoid unpleasantness.
- Never run checkpoints; never display maps openly.
- Carry a short-wave radio to keep track of developments on the BBC or other reliable stations.
- Think through your mission, how best to get the story. For example, do you risk sniper fire or should you be more circumspect?
- Keep an active mind regarding risks and ask yourself questions.
- All you have in dangerous situations are your wits and knowledge of the area. Your editor and the Geneva Convention normally can't help you.
- Make certain you know the local meaning of symbols like white flags, red flags, whistles, gestures, etc.
- Evaluate your physical characteristics. Don't attempt something you lack stamina to complete.
- Make certain your employer carries insurance that will adequately provide if you are injured or killed.
- Editors should always be aware of the risks reporters or photographers are running. They also bear responsibility and should not push unreasonably.

Reproduced from *Journalists on Dangerous Assignments*, edited by Louis Falls Montgomery, International Press Institute, 1986.

The Anchor

No matter how distinguished or respected reporters may appear to their peers and to the public, there is no doubt that the glamour and fame associated with television journalism attaches more to those who regularly present news or news-related programmes. The curiosity is that the newscaster, newsreader, presenter, anchor – whatever the title – has not always been a journalist. Readers are known to have been hired for their looks or voices and have not necessarily even been invited to make any contribution towards the editorial process, their liberty to change scripts – only after due consultation – being confined to words or phrases they find difficult to say.

The journalist/presenter

The arrival of the journalist as presenter has coincided with new demands created by technological change and the introduction of modern programme formats. Journalistic and presentational skills have become inseparable. Now, when executives look for people able to meet this dual requirement they turn first to their more experienced reporters, some of whom are weary after years of being on the road and are prepared to exchange their globe-trotting for the safety of the studio and elevation to star status. So journalist/presenters are hired not for their looks or voices alone, but also for their experience, and as a consequence are able to command salaries far in excess of the programme editors to whom in theory they may be junior.

Presenter power

Where proper chains of command are not established, collisions of ego are not unknown, usually to the detriment of the programme. Some managements believe that this 'creative tension' makes a positive contribution towards lively journalism. Other organisations do not allow reporters to become presenters for more than short periods, while others try to avoid the problem altogether by making the reporter/presenter the editor, adding executive responsibility for budgets, and the assigning, hiring and firing of staff to the day-to-day editorial decision making. This may be effective policy at one level, but as soon as transmission time approaches and the manager/presenter has to become only the presenter, the difficulties become apparent, leading to the creation of enormous strains on a single person, whatever their talents.

This problem is not likely to surface for the new reporter, but if you have a secret yearning for the presenter's chair, volunteer for a few programmes as a reader at weekends and see if you can establish a reputation as a reliable stand-in. Who knows where that might lead?

In the Studio

The prospect of anchoring a news programme under the bright lights of a television studio in front of millions of critical viewers is enough to make anyone apprehensive.

Although they may never admit it, even the most experienced news presenters suffer an occasional attack of 'butterflies' before a programme. On location there is the possibility of a face-saving second take: in the studio there is no reprieve. The wrong inflection, the slight hesitation or stumble over a word, the sidelong glance or twitch of a facial muscle is a matter for comment and discussion.

Thriving under pressure
Being at the centre of a hectic, live programme may be exactly the right role if you are one of those who thrives on pressure and responsibility.

Accept also that it can be a lonely occupation. You may be expected to operate entirely on your own from a tiny, out-of-town studio equipped with only a remote-controlled camera and lights you switch on yourself to broadcast to the unseen audience.

Glitzy presentation in bigger studios may not offer much more company. You may be asked to read from a computer-driven script-prompting device mounted on robotic cameras, introduce a succession of recorded images played from another part of the building and listen to the disembodied voice of the studio director shouting in your ear. The nearest human contact may be the floor manager standing well out of camera range.

In your own words...
What you may find most difficult is the idea that what you are reading has been written by someone else. Ten to one you will not be happy with the style or the phrasing. And here it depends how much authority the reader has – either to alter material written by others, or to write it yourself. Even if you wished, it is unlikely that you would be able to write an entire half-hour programme. The concession many programmes make to their journalist/presenters is to allow them to write the headlines, if there are any, or perhaps the opening item.

...and those of others
At the very least the opportunity is likely to occur for you to see every script before it is finalised so that a certain amount of personal authority can be injected. The trick is to encourage others to write in 'your' style right from the beginning or, if that is not possible, to make alterations in a way which retains accuracy and allows the originator of the material to keep some professional pride. Complaints that you have ruined scripts by making alterations without consultation will not enhance your reputation with the rest of the team.

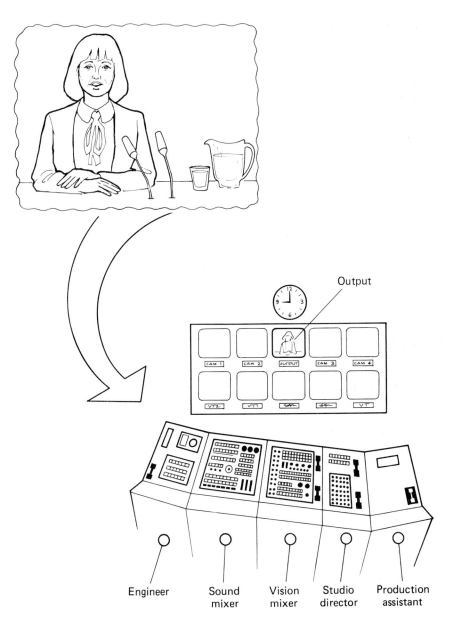

Engineer | Sound mixer | Vision mixer | Studio director | Production assistant

In the studio
The television studio can be a lonely place. Instructions to the presenter are fed from a control room probably some distance away. The studio director (1) is in charge of the production team, which may include a production assistant (2), technicians in charge of vision (3) and sound (4), and a senior engineer (5)

115

Perfecting Posture

Among the most common faults of those facing the studio television camera is that of poor posture. Some readers slouch back in their chairs, others – unable to sit squarely – thrust one shoulder forwards in a seemingly aggressive manner which also presents only one eye to the audience. Other readers are so nervous that they sit literally on the seat edge, or slump so round-shouldered that they fill only the bottom of the screen. Still more fidget. All of these habits are distractions. What the viewers want to see is you, the presenter, looking relaxed, confident and assured. Don't let them spend time wondering what is wrong. They will not be able to concentrate on the important matters which you have to tell and show them, and they will become irritated, bored, and switch off.

The wriggle routine
Develop a short routine you go through before you settle down to read a script. First, wriggle yourself comfortably into your chair. If – as in the majority of news-type programmes – there is a desk between yourself and the camera, make sure the chair is at a height which suits your physique and not that of the giant who used it last. If it cannot be adjusted, ask for another.

Check that you are exactly far enough away to put down and pick up your papers naturally, without stretching. Don't worry about the cameras. It is the responsibility of the production staff to move them if necessary. Above all, do not allow yourself to be rushed.

If you still have a tendency to slump, try sitting on your coat tail to keep your back straight. If you are not in the habit of wearing a coat, write in large letters at the top of your script 'sit up straight'.

Using a clipboard
The more informal the programme, the more difficulties there often are for the presenter, who is likely to have to cope with a wad of script pages in one hand and a favourite pen or pencil in the other. If there are no desks or tables within easy reach, cross your legs and rest the papers on your knee. If there are many pages do not risk getting them out of order or spilling them on the floor – you don't want to be scrambling among the camera cables just before an important interview.

The best tip is to keep your sheets on a clipboard, turning them over with the hand which holds the pen. Sheets can be discarded out of shot during the programme.

116

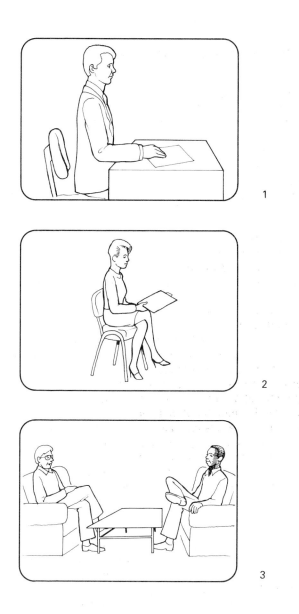

1

2

3

Formality and informality
Posture is important: try sitting on your coat tails to keep your back straight (1). If there's no desk you'll have to balance your script on your knee, but it can be difficult to sit elegantly (2). Informal sets have easy chairs and coffee tables (3).

The Script Prompter

One of the great innovations towards helping television performers improve their technique in the studio has been the introduction of prompting devices which give the impression that words are being spoken from memory.

These aids have become sophisticated and unobtrusive enough for others to find a use for them, for they add a professional touch as well as giving confidence and credibility to all forms of speech-making. The prompter has become a lifeline for any self-respecting reader who does not wish to present the audience with a regular view of the top of the head.

Beyond the idiot board

Script-prompting hardware has improved considerably since the first 'idiot boards', handwritten cards or sheets held just below or to one side of the camera. The 'idiot' was the reader who was presumably unable to memorise the words of an item or entire programme. The effectiveness of this simple method was marred by the difficulty of keeping the boards positioned so the reader's look did not stray annoyingly off camera.

Although 'idiot boards' of one kind or another are still in use, new systems more in keeping with the advances made elsewhere in television journalism have been introduced.

The most advanced have the words reflected by a mirror device which fits the front of each camera without obscuring the lens. The reader looks directly into it – and therefore towards the audience – while speaking. The other half of the system usually consists of a tiny television camera operated by a member of the production team in a corner of the studio. The camera scans the script, which is placed under it page by page, magnifying the words. As a variant the script can be retyped onto a narrow roll of paper which the operator feeds through at a pace to match the speaker's reading speed.

Computer links

The most modern types, portable enough for field use, can be linked to the newsroom computer systems which started to become commonplace in the mid-1980s. In this way scripts written in the newsroom are generated electronically, appearing in front of the reader at the push of a button, the advantage being that stories can be rewritten or updated in an instant. So theoretically, studio performers are able to read straight from their 'prompter' screens, but most prefer the security of having solid paper scripts in their hands, just in case something suddenly goes wrong with the electronics.

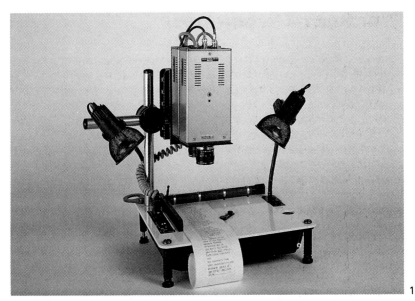

Script-prompting

Electronic script-prompting devices allow the presenter to look straight at the audience while reading. In this system a tiny television camera scans the script fed under it at a speed regulated by hand or remote control or by foot pedal. The drive accepts any paper width from 8 cm prompter roll to 24 cm computer stationery (1). The words of the script are displayed on a unit which is fitted to the camera without obscuring the lens (2) (courtesy Broadcast Developments Ltd, Autoscript)

Prompter Techniques

Being an effective user of any studio prompter device is not simply a matter of staring glassily into the correct camera and reading whatever appears on the screen. Nervous newcomers have a tendency to think of a prompting device as a life-support system which they dare not let go of, forgetting that it is just another tool.

Most devices display only about half a dozen lines at a time. A tiny arrow in the left-hand corner usually points to the second line – the one above has always just been read and is about to disappear from the top of the screen, those below are moving from the bottom into line of sight. In some particularly sophisticated systems the reader's measured reading speed is programmed into a computer so that the words appear at an automatically even pace. More usually it is the operator who follows the reader, speeding up or slowing down the movement as appropriate.

Avoid the shifty look

Where the script has been retyped, the narrowness of the paper restricts the number of the words on each line to no more than six or seven. The aim is to encourage reading without the perceptible eye or head movements which can look shifty. Make a point of trying to read the words from the centre of the screen rather than from side to side. On occasions during a longish stint in front of the camera, move your weight slightly: it will make you look less like a robot.

The same purpose is behind the technique of looking down occasionally to consult a script. Although viewers are aware that no reader can possibly have learned everything by heart, they sometimes need to be reassured that some facts – figures, especially – are not somehow being conjured out of the air. So the trick is to look down as if refreshing the memory, then to look up and continue reading.

Keeping your place

The difficult bit is ensuring that you do not lose your place on the prompter. This is not as easy as it seems, as the practice in some organisations is to type out only those parts of the script which are intended to be read to camera. The rest consists of words to be read out of vision, behind graphics for example. On a busy night with last-minute changes being made to the script, it is all too easy to go wrong.

Finally, a simple remedy for those who cannot read the prompter comfortably without leaning forward – get glasses.

The electronic prompter
(1) Reader's eye view (courtesy EDS Portaprompt). (2) Prompting systems linked with newsroom computers allow script changes and updates to be made without writers leaving their desks for the studio (courtesy Autocue)

A custom-made earpiece will fit better.

Talkback

Another part of the art of presenting in the studio comes with listening to what is going on in the control room. 'Talkback' gives you direct contact with the director or editor, so instructions before or during any programme item can be given easily. Using the desk telephone always looks so theatrical.

Almost every regular studio performer of any status is now equipped with a tiny, snug-fitting personal earpiece, rather like a hearing-aid. The other end is fitted to a long cable which eventually plugs into an electrical socket at the back of the desk.

You may find it impossible to use this device at first: it's rather like the childish game of trying to pat your head and rub your stomach at the same time. It takes practice to concentrate on speaking clearly while people in another room are chattering excitedly in your ear, often about matters which do not strictly concern you.

On the other hand it is a splendidly useful means of communication. For example, many readers like to be counted in and out of video inserts, relying on the warning voice of the production assistant in their ear, and there is more than one star television performer who has cause to be thankful for this mechanism which allows an astute producer in the control room to regularly whisper the line of questioning to be followed during live interviews.

Although the word 'talkback' implies a two-way process, the only way you are able to talk back to the control room is by using the desk microphone. If you do, make sure it's not 'live', during transmission.

The floor manager
If you prefer, the distractions of talkback can be avoided by switching it off during transmission and putting your faith in the floor manager, who is linked by headset and microphone to the control room.

The floor manager stands out of camera range but near enough to be able to relay the studio director's instructions by hand signals. In many cases these may consist of nothing more complicated than a series of rehearsed finger movements to denote the time remaining on a video insert. In other cases the floor manager has an essential role in the progress of live interviews or other items which need to be kept strictly to their planned duration, and so circular 'wind-up' and 'cut-throat' actions are used as time runs out.

The floor manager
The floor manager acts as the link between the control room and the presenter in the studio (courtesy BBC Central Stills)

Too cosy a partnership will seem phoney.

Presenters in Partnership

The preference for news-related programmes to be fronted by one, two or more presenters is influenced as much by fashion as by journalistic needs. Changes are quite often made as part of the acceptable, periodic revision of format or style made by all long-running factual programmes, and a decision to switch from, say, solo to dual presentation – or viceversa – is treated as one element of a revamp or re-launch likely to include the introduction of new sets, titles, music and graphics.

Sometimes it goes beyond the cosmetic: a multi-presentation format may be driven by the need to base anchors in different centres, to inject pace and variety, or to relieve the pressures on a single journalist fronting longer, technically complicated programmes.

Attracting the audience
Male–female partnerships are particularly popular with audiences, and other combinations intended to broaden the viewing base include teams which have an age or racial mix.

Dividing the work
Where presenters are in tandem the aim is usually to split the work more or less equally (some insist on a minimum share of on-air time being written into their contracts). As a standby or novice presenter it is unlikely that you would be in a position to make similar demands, but from the outset it is worth clarifying the extent of your contribution: whether you are expected to conduct interviews during the programme, or read alternate segments, scripts or voice-overs. This is a wise precaution, as it is not unknown for 'junior' presenters to find themselves disadvantaged by their established star partners, who feel threatened and attempt to influence programme managements to divide the reading spoils in a way which gives them the hard news and serious political interviews and leaves you with all the soft items.

Formality and informality
Journalists never cease to argue about the degree of informality which ought to exist between presenter partnerships on air. Of course it depends on so many things, one being the time a programme is being transmitted. Breakfast news-show styles tend to be the most relaxed, with formality seeming to increase progressively through the day.

My own view is that presenters should convey a friendly yet crisp and efficient impression to the audience without descending to the jocularity and byplay which rarely comes across as anything but contrived.

If you are encouraged to be informal, be aware that on occasions it can seem callous and badly out of place. The end of a programme made up of a catalogue of death and disaster is no time for merry quips between presenters.

In tandem
Team presentation calls for the audience to believe that two people are sharing the same studio, even though they may be seen together only briefly at the opening and closing of a programme. For this it is essential to maintain an interest when it is not your turn. As your partner finishes an item the camera should find you looking in his or her direction. The hint of a head turn towards the audience will add to the impression that the two of you are working together.

Play fair by your interviewee.

Studio Interviewing (1)

The arrival of the journalist/presenter or anchor has meant a broadening of the role beyond the straightforward reading to camera. Live studio interviews within news programmes are no longer the novelties they once were, and anyone aspiring to a permanent studio-based role needs to develop the technique.

The difference between interviewing on location and in a studio is more than a matter of the difference between a live broadcast and an edited recording. Transferred to the confines of a studio, almost any interview appears to take on a more confrontational nature, created in part by the technical paraphernalia of cameras and lights, which add an air of unreality to the proceedings.

The interviewer's test
Your skill in interviewing live is tested to the full by the need to:
- Make the interview flow.
- Extract the best from the subject as a duty to the audience.
- Avoid making grammatical or editorial errors which cannot be corrected.
- Cover all the relevant ground before the interview runs its allotted duration.

This task is rarely made easier by the interview subject. Canny, ring-wise politicians have the ability to make mincemeat of interviewers if they have a mind to do so.

Part of your difficulty with these interviews is a natural tendency to play fair by your visitors and not to appear aggressive, so those who have developed the infuriating but devastating technique of ignoring your questions and answering their own can be very hard to put in their place.

An added drawback is that the public usually relishes the sight of an interviewer on the retreat. Equally, many big-name interviewers become as famous as those who regularly make the headlines, and the gladiatorial nature of an interview between people who socialise off-screen can sometimes be no more than play-acting. That much is often made clear by their behaviour towards each other before or after the event.

Interview one plus one
Most live interviews in the studio are between two people. The set should be designed so they face more or less opposite. If they sit side-by-side they will be looking towards each other in profile and the audience will seem to be excluded. Camera positioning should be such that the subject talks to both the interviewer and the audience. This is best achieved with a three-camera set-up: one trained on the interviewer, one on the interviewee, and one on a two-shot of both.

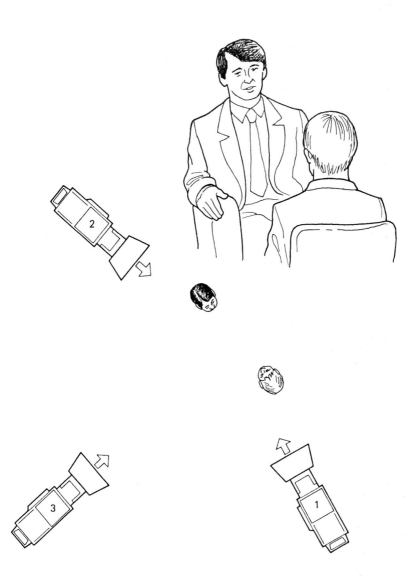

Interview one plus one
A three-camera set-up. Camera 1 is trained on the interviewee, Camera 2 on you and Camera 3 covers both participants in a two-shot.

Studio Interviewing (2)

Interview one plus two

Conducting an interview with two people is obviously twice as tricky as with one, chiefly because of the need to play fair by each participant. For even if the two interviewees are theoretically on 'the same side', it is important that both should have their say, as much for the sake of good television as for balance.

It is not always enough to ask each the same question in turn: this can be far too slow and predictable. The interviewer's skill comes in being able to pick up one answer and use it to move the subject smoothly forward, so by the end of the allotted time a satisfactory amount of ground has been covered and a range of interviews heard.

Firmness counts

Where the participants have strongly opposing views it is important not to let the interview become a succession of claims and counter-claims. Resist the temptation to deliberately light the fuse and retire to enjoy the fireworks. Although a good row between interviewees can produce spectacular viewing, it is just as likely to degenerate into childishness which quickly becomes very boring. Far better not to let things get out of control from the beginning. Firmness is essential, otherwise you may find yourself a virtual spectator as the 'ball' is batted across from one side to the other. Assert your authority as politely as possible, making sure you do not appear to be in favour of one or other of the arguments.

Setting up the studio for the one plus two may be less problematical than may seem obvious. If three cameras are available, one can cover both speakers in single shots if they sit opposite you side-by-side. But it is important to have separate microphones for each person.

Interview one plus more than two

It is arguable whether multi-participant interviews are of much editorial value within a news-type programme of limited duration. There never seems to be enough time available to give everyone a decent hearing. From a production point of view, too, such interviews can be difficult unless a proper set has been built to accommodate large numbers.

On the rare occasions when you are faced with interviews of this type, take time out from your research to help advise on seating arrangements. Without preparation, the production team will be unable to direct the cameras and microphones at the right people when they speak.

One plus two
An unusual combination: one interviewer and two interviewees. Sky News, launched in February 1989, recruited politicians with opposing views – Norman Tebbit (Conservative) and Austin Mitchell (Labour) – to quiz guests for a regular programme (courtesy Sky News)

Live interview dos

- DO know your subject. There's no better way of keeping your interviewee's respect and interest.

- DO prepare your questions in advance.

- DO listen to the answers and be ready with supplementaries.

- DO wait for a breath pause or natural break in speech flow if you have to interrupt.

- DO keep the interviewee to the subject under discussion.

- DO be persistent if you can't get answers to legitimate questions. But judge when enough is enough.

- DO not be tempted to defer to an interviewee who is famous or powerful.

- DO nurture the nervous. If an interviewee has a tendency to avoid eye-contact ask a direct question to attract greater attention.

- DO give time for thought: silence can be telling.

- Do keep control of your facial expressions. Raising your eyebrows or nodding your head could be interpreted as comment.

- DO remember that it's your job to ask questions, not to take part in a debate.

- DO avoid putting words into people's mouths: 'What I think you are trying to say, Mr Bloggs, is. . .'

- DO remember who you are interviewing. 'Drying' is quite natural under pressure. Write the subject's name and title on your script.

- DO listen to control-room talkback.

- DO try to pace yourself so the interview comes to a smooth conclusion.

- DO keep to the time you have been allotted. Finishing earlier or later than planned will disturb programme balance.

- DO remember you have the privilege of being able to ask the questions the average person would like to put, given the opportunity. You are representing the audience, no-one else.

Live interview don'ts

- DON'T assume the audience shares any specialist knowledge you may have.

- DON'T stick rigidly to prepared questions and ignore the answers.

- DON'T make statements. The interviewee may not know when to answer.

- DON'T make statements of your own in the form of questions. You aren't taking part in a debate.

- DON'T as a rule refer to interviewees by their first names: it can sound patronising.

- DON'T talk at the same time as your subject.

- DON'T bicker or lose your temper under provocation.

- DON'T be intimidated by an overbearing interviewee.

- DON'T bully or hector an interviewee who is unimportant or inarticulate.

- DON'T go easy on someone just because you sympathise.

- DON'T jump in with another question if an interviewee hesitates: allow a few seconds for recovery.

- DON'T let your own opinions come through. No-one is interested.

- DON'T respond to answers with 'I see', 'yes' or semi-audible grunts. It could be habit-forming.

- DON'T ask leading questions: '. . . and then I believe you saw the fire-engine coming round the corner at sixty miles an hour. . .'

- DON'T enter into little intimacies or conspiracies with the interviewee to the exclusion of the viewer. 'You and I both remember what happened after that wonderful meal in Paris. . .but we'd better not talk about that, ha, ha.'

- DON'T ignore the floor-manager's signals. They are there to help you.

- DON'T cut your interviewee off with a brusque 'Sorry, we are out of time.'

- DON'T FORGET that you have the privilege of being able to ask the questions the average person would like to put, given the opportunity. You are representing the audience, no-one else.

Dealing with Tricky Customers

Although the advantages might all appear to be on the side of the professional television interviewer operating on familiar home ground, there is a common belief among journalists that the initiative is rapidly passing to the experienced interviewee who knows how to exploit the system. Pressure may be brought to bear before, during or after the event – perhaps at all three stages. In some cases it can be interpreted as no more than an interviewee's genuine and understandable anxiety to be seen in the best light; in others it can be a justifiable attempt to win fair treatment. On a worryingly large number it adds up to blatant news management.

The blunt
Much of the pressure is straightforward and unsubtle. It usually consists of one or several conditions laid down before an interviewee will agree to appear at all. Among the most frequent demands made are those to do with submission of questions in advance, a request for no editing, or at least approval before transmission, and questions of payment.

Occasionally the interviewee will try to stipulate who conducts the interview or attempt to exercise a veto over other participants, and it should not come as a surprise if new conditions are made by an interviewee on the brink of an appearance as a means of exerting additional pressure. There's nothing like the threat of a last-minute walk-out by the star interviewee to make the most determined reporter revise questions.

The subtle
Some interviewees in regular demand, often people holding important public office, are well aware of the influence they wield. They know the programmes and people likely to provide them with the best exposure, and will make themselves available – or not – accordingly. They also learn enough about the mechanics of television programme making to be able to exploit the complicated arrangements sometimes necessary to mount items. They know a 'few hours' delay in answering a harassed producer's request for an interview can be turned to their advantage, especially if their presence depends on that of others.

Interview training
Many of the best exponents of interviewee technique have been instructed by professional journalists hired to offer training in the art of facing the camera. There is often more to it than tuition in how to evade awkward questions. Those who are likely to appear regularly are advised on posture, delivery and dress. Anyone considered not to be telegenic may be told to keep off the screen altogether in their belief that the viewer is more likely to be won over by the personable and articulate.

Before the interview

These are among the conditions interviewees are known to have laid down before agreeing to be interviewed:

SOLO INTERVIEWS
Non-appearance unless:
- 'live' transmission
- guaranteed position in programme
- duration agreed
- questions submitted in advance
- approval of interviewer
- preview of any other contributions
- no editing of recording
- preview and approval of recording before transmission

MULTIPLE INTERVIEWS
Non-appearance unless:
- veto over other participants
- guarantee of minimum time
- guarantee of the 'last word'
- veto over seating arrangements

Other ploys:
- threats to leave before interview
- intimidation of the interviewer

During the interview
- evasion of questions
- insistence on making statements
- interruptions
- calling by Christian name
- simulated anger
- walk-out

After the interview
- complaint about treatment
- insistence on apology
- insistence on vetting recording
- threat of legal action

Difficult interviewees
It is quite legitimate for interviewees to lay down conditions before they agree to appear, although be on your guard against anything which smacks of news manipulation. In the end it depends on how badly you want the interview. But once you have agreed to any conditions, stick to them.

Interviewee on the Attack

It would be wrong to assume that all interviews for television are arranged with mutual respect and a proper regard for the needs of both sides, bearing in mind that in the end they are providing a service for the viewer. Alas, it is not like that at times. Interminable wrangling over seemingly trivial detail goes on behind the scenes before the participants ever reach the studio, although it has to be emphasised that what we are considering here are mainly news-related or potentially contentious items and not talk shows or other forms of entertainment interview.

Softening up the interviewer

Sometimes a strong performance on television does wonders for a politician's waning popularity – as much with their peers as with the voter – and it is understandable that they should try to seize any psycho-logical advantage which offers itself. Don't be caught off-guard by pre-interview tactics. These might include half-joking, half-serious criticism of your past work, complaints about real or imagined transgressions on the part of colleagues or your parent news organisation.

Ignoring the question

At some time or other during an interview of significance, the experienced interviewee is likely to introduce the favourite yet effective ploy of ignoring your question and answering one of their own. Fortunately, most signal what's coming well in advance with a reply which says, in essence: 'I really think you're missing the point. What's far more important...'

Other interviewees do not bother with such subtleties. Instead they deliberately go off at a tangent or create an impenetrable verbal smoke-screen through which it is practically impossible to judge whether the question has been answered at all. If you are not careful the interview can be beyond control in no time.

Be patient. Repeat the question and, if necessary, say why you are doing so. As long as you are courteous and don't appear to be over-zealous, the audience will be on your side.

Other ploys

Another favourite ploy is to patronise the interviewer by using his or her first name. It is extremely difficult to ask hard questions of someone who seems anxious to be friendly and co-operative. Counter this by using the appropriate honorific.

Post-interview troubles

Even if an interview has apparently gone well, it is no guarantee against unwelcome complaint from those who have had second thoughts about what they should or should not have said. Protests that a recorded interview has been distorted through editing should be taken seriously.

Tricky customers
An imaginary television interview in Three Acts.

BACKGROUND: the government's treatment of the economy has hit a rough patch and there are calls for the resignation of those responsible for policy. One senior politician whose position is known to be vulnerable has agreed to a live interview on a daily current affairs programme.

ACT ONE: BEFORE TRANSMISSION
(Scene, an anteroom. Politician is being attended to by a make-up artist while discussing the subject with interviewer, an experienced television reporter. They know each other well.)

POL. Now Bill, you know I'm always happy to co-operate, but you're not going to ask any trick questions, are you?
INT. Well John, obviously I am going to have to ask you generally about the state of the economy and then, more specifically, whether you think there will have to be a change of direction. You know your position is a bit vulnerable.
POL. You're telling me! But don't overstate it. No-one's going to thank you for trying to undermine confidence in what we are doing. Just the same, I don't see why I should sacrifice my political career for the sake of some incompetent computer programmer.
INT. Come on, you know they'll look after you. Anyway, I'm going to have to ask the question.
POL (gloomily). I daresay. But I don't promise to answer.

ACT TWO: IN THE STUDIO
(The interview is under way.)

INT. Mr Jones, the government's own figures show that things aren't going as well as it had forecast. What do you think has gone wrong?
POL. Well, Bill, you and I know the question which should really be addressed is why the previous administration allowed the situation to get so far out of hand it has taken this long to get matters under control.
INT. Isn't it that the situation was being remedied but that you have simply been blown off course?
POL. If you knew anything about economics you'd know that even the most effective policies and the strongest economies are affected by industrial demand and trading patterns in the rest of the world. Surely you'll accept we've made tremendous advances in the past few years.
INT. Mr Jones, what's your reply to those critics inside the government who don't accept that advances have been made and say it is time to introduce new ideas and new people to implement them?
POL. I told you before we began this interview, Bill, that I was not going to answer that question should you put it to me. But I see that as usual the media is not interested in issues, only the unfounded gossip and rumour to do with personalities.
INT. Mr Jones, I'll put it this way. Do you think it is right for the country's economic policy to be in the hands of those in whom some members of the government appear to have lost confidence?
POL. Bill, we are both old hands at this game. It is quite irresponsible of you to go on attempting to ask a question to which I have already given an answer.
INT. But you have refused to answer it, haven't you?
POL. I have answered your question by saying that I am not going to comment on rumour and speculation about my position. So I suggest you change the subject. . .

ACT THREE: AFTER THE INTERVIEW
(Scene, the hospitality room.)

POL (cheerily). Well, I think that went rather well Bill, don't you? Thanks. Now, what about that drink. . .

Audience Participation

Most traditional news-type programmes are serious affairs conducted within the confines of some kind of studio. The public 'out there' is kept on the other side of the television set.

But some of the most charismatic and experienced presenter/reporters who have demonstrated an ability to meet more taxing challenges are invited to host shows in which the participation of an audience is an essential ingredient.

'Panel' programmes which lend themselves to this form of treatment are held in studios or sizeable halls. They are usually fairly relaxed and informal, although the topics they cover – social and environmental issues, health, politics, for example – are serious enough. Each tries to offer something unique in the way of presentation, but the format is now pretty well established and only cosmetic differences are readily apparent.

Programme format

A typical format for one of these programmes consists of two or more groups chosen by the producer or editor for their opposing views, and an audience made up of supporters and neutrals. Questions may be prearranged or come spontaneously from the studio/hall audience or viewers. You may be seated on a platform at one end, facing the audience, or the 'stage' may be located in the middle as if in a theatre in the round.

As the host, it is up to you to allow the main players to espouse their cause (within reason), score points off each other, answer the audience's questions positively, and entertain at the same time. You also have to intervene on occasions to 'referee', seek clarification, chide the question side-steppers, take a firm grip on speakers who attempt to hog the proceedings, and – unless it is 'timeless' – be conscious of the clock.

Be prepared

These programmes are transmitted live, some recorded 'as live' without editing. Others are recorded an hour or so before transmission to allow trimming to time. They are intended to be as much entertainment as good journalism, so approach them in that spirit.

If the programme is meant to reflect current topics, be up to date on what is important. Most journalists invariably are, though even the best can be caught out at times. At the minimum, preparation should consist of a few newspaper clippings put aside for possible use in an emergency. Research the main characters before the programme. If it is one of a series, you may expect to meet the main participants over a meal at which the broad outline of subjects can be discussed. It provides an opportunity for the less experienced to relax without spoiling spontaneity.

Audience participation
Audiences have an integral part in some programmes. The test for the host is to
keep the questions and answers flowing and not to let any one person dominate
the proceedings. 'Kilroy', this programme, is hosted by a former politician,
Robert Kilroy-Silk (courtesy BBC Central Stills)

Talk Shows

Not all talk show hosts have a background in journalism. Not all journalists aspire to hosting talk shows. But it is not difficult to see how the skills needed for news and current affairs can be adapted to lengthier, interview-based programmes for television or radio.

The set
In purely televisual terms, live talk shows (or chat shows – call them what you will) are simple, unsophisticated programmes. The set usually consists of a chair for the interviewer and a settee or easy chairs for the guests. Interviews often start off as one to one, with other visitors brought in to join the conversation, so that by the end of thirty or forty minutes the interviewer is having to deal with four or five people – no easy task, sometimes, when everyone wants to have the first and last word.

That's entertainment
Even more than audience participation programmes, talk shows are firmly entertainment-based, and 'star' hosts are often derided for the salaries they command. But these programmes are far harder than they look. They stand or fall on the ability of the interviewer to extract worthwhile conversation from subjects who may turn out to be boring, inarticulate, sulking, drunk, even – in extremes – violent.

Journalistic intuition will tell you how far you can go in pursuit of embarrassing or irrelevant topics. Some shows thrive on controversy. If that's intentional, fine. But if your brief is to keep things light and frothy, don't step outside it.

The guests
Presenters of shows are usually supported by teams of researchers who beaver away at finding interesting guests. Having done so they should ensure that you are fully and accurately briefed.

Some shows have a topical flavour. Guests may be vaguely 'in the news' or known to be 'available' from a list of names circulated by agents, hotels or airlines anxious to publicise the activity of star clientele.

Celebrities who for most of the year say they are too busy to appear on television suddenly find themselves available when they are about to open in a new play or publish a book. Then it becomes a merry-go-round of appearances on a succession of similar programmes in a very short space of time.

Critics sometimes complain that talk shows can be influenced by agents or publicists who wish to see their clients on the screen, and play off one programme against another to get the best deal, the most time, the highest rated programme and the most popular or compliant host. Programme editors should think carefully before deciding how far guests should be allowed to plug their latest commercial activities.

Talk shows
The aim is relaxed informality and entertaining conversation between star interviewers and their guests. Terry Wogan (1) for the BBC and Frank Bough (2) for Sky News (courtesy BBC Central Stills, Sky News)

Phone-ins

Phone-ins tend to be thought of as a recent popular phenomenon. Although it is a technique more appropriate to radio, where hours of cheap programming can be obtained by asking listeners to ring in (often at their own expense) on all manner of subjects, phone-ins have a long history of exposure on television as well. (BBC Archives record a television phone-in for a Party Political Broadcast in July, 1954.)

Series of phone-in programmes have been established, many a skilful mix of part studio-based, part telephone questioning. Politics, social and consumer affairs, and listeners' letters are just a few of the topics which lend themselves readily to the treatment, and once you have been enrolled as a host, voluntarily or otherwise, you are likely to find yourself in charge of lengthy live programmes, frequently in the small hours.

Achieving balance

The simplest phone-ins are those which find you alone, fielding calls from the public on some stated topic. In others you will have to cope with a guest or two, a studio audience, and a succession of incoming calls. The skill here is to juggle all elements, keeping the programme flowing in the gaps between calls.

Probably you will have help behind the scenes. Potential contributors speak first to a researcher/producer about the point they wish to raise. In this way repetition is avoided, a balance can be kept between arguments, and new or associated topics introduced. This is also an early warning against callers likely to let loose a stream of abuse or obscenities on the air. Some programmes have a built-in recording device which delays the question long enough for someone to intercept. Bona fide callers are asked to wait or are telephoned back when their turn comes.

Concentrate on the caller

Your role is to act as go-between, interposing when necessary to ensure the caller receives a proper answer. Some contributors become tongue-tied the moment they are invited to put their question, and you should come to the rescue, interpreting or clarifying as the need arises. The caller must not be allowed to seem foolish or be left uncertain about when to speak. Contributors' names are probably fed to you through your ear-piece, or on a television monitor out of sight of the viewing audience, but make a habit of writing down who each caller is, where he or she comes from, and the gist of the question. It might save embarrassment. Allow supplementaries and try not to cut people off abruptly. Thanking a caller politely for their contribution is a neat way of telling them their time has run out.

Above all, don't panic .

When Things go Wrong

Not even the most experienced professional presenter is immune from the potential disasters which lurk, waiting to strike every live television programme. Modern technology may not be as vulnerable to breakdown as in the past, but there is still plenty to go wrong. Computer systems crash, cameras go 'on the blink', lights fail – always, of course, at the most inopportune moments. Satellite links which worked perfectly during technical line-up moments before transmission develop mysterious faults, leaving no time for substitutes or replacements to be found. Video inserts come up with picture but no sound, or sound but no picture; or the right pictures with the wrong sound, and vice versa. The electronic prompting device jams.

Then there is the human element. 'Finger trouble' is the euphemism for any production error which causes, say, the vision mixer in the control gallery to mistake the intended shot on Camera One (close-up of Female Star Presenter) for the shot on Camera Two (close-up of Male Star Presenter picking his teeth). Scripts written too late to meet their deadline are every news programme editor's nightmare. Scripts may be written in time but the accompanying video report may be unfinished. The guest interviewee may not arrive because the taxi driver sent to collect him went to the wrong rendezvous. 'Over now to our reporter at the White House/Number Ten Downing Street/the State Department/Union head-quarters' – but the screen is empty.

Unwelcome intruders
Intruders protesting about minority rights evade studio security and chain themselves to a camera at the start of a network news programme watched by millions. The main presenter calmly continues the newscast as if nothing has happened while her male partner muffles the shouts of one demonstrator with the seat of his trousers.

Keep calm
The only thing to do when catastrophe strikes is to keep calm. Apologies sometimes seem in order, although one school of thought says it is pointless to draw attention to some minor technical fault that the non-expert viewer would probably not notice. At the other extreme it is foolish to ignore a succession of obvious calamities by pretending they have not happened. Usually the studio control room will come to the rescue with instructions through your earpiece or, in some cases, the emergency telephone on the desk. Quite often the common sense approach is to go on to the next item as soon as possible while the technicalities are sorted out behind the scenes.

But the worst thing presenters can do is to give the impression that it is somehow nothing to do with them and what has gone wrong with the programme is the result of inefficiency elsewhere. That is unforgivable.

Treat your guests with tact and courtesy.

Last Words on Interviewing

And finally . . . remember interviewees are your guests. The way they are treated will determine their attitude towards you and your organisation, and whether – if they are worth cultivating – they are likely to accept a future invitation to appear. It's of benefit to you that they turn up at the right place at the right time. Do not invite interviewees to appear unless you genuinely intend to use them. It is discourteous in the extreme.

Inevitably, there will be occasions when editorial considerations mean 'dropping' at the last moment a guest who has taken considerable trouble to join you. Apologise profusely.

To pay or not to pay?
Guests who take part in news programmes do not usually expect to be paid, although you cannot assume everyone is able to give up their time for nothing. If an interviewee would otherwise be out of pocket it is not unreasonable to offer a small 'disturbance fee' by way of compensation, travelling expenses, or company transport.

Looking after your guest
Do not ignore interviewees when they arrive. If you cannot meet the guest yourself, make it a rule to have someone available to guide them to the studio or a waiting room. Let them know what is happening and when they are expected to appear. Offer hospitality: it need be no more than a cup of coffee.

On the air
Be polite, certainly, but do not overdo the verbal greetings. They are inclined to slow down the proceedings. Some nervous interviewees cannot stop talking: when you want to interrupt, make sure they see you lean forward. Others look away when answering. Proper chair positioning will help: otherwise ask a direct question which will make them look at you. Ensure fidgety interviewees are not given swivel chairs. They will probably swivel out of shot.

Illustrating the interview
If you intend to illustrate the interview with graphics, video, or items brought in by the guest (this often happens with magazine programmes) be sure there is time to prepare: the studio will need to set up separate camera shots or lighting changes. If there is any chance illustrations may not appear at the right time or seem out of place – forget them.

How you say goodbye...
. . . is as important as how you say hello. You don't have to say 'thank you' on screen, but make sure you do privately afterwards. Then, if it is possible, offer hospitality and return transport.

Looking after your guests

Studio interviewees may be difficult to stop talking. If you don't want to interrupt them in full flight, leaning forward (1) should indicate your intention. If it falls within your responsibility to position studio guests, make sure fidgets are not seated in swivel chairs. They might swivel out of shot (2).

Your chance to jump off the tramlines.

Documentaries

Television documentaries present journalists with opportunities to explore subjects in greater depth and length than is normal with news or news-related programmes. More than that, some are 'signed', allowing the reporter to set aside the impartiality demanded of everyday programming in favour of a rarely expressed personal view.

Shape and content

The documentary has no set agenda, so shape, content and duration are open to individual interpretation. Its scope is considerable, and that is why so many imaginative reporters, tramlined by the constraints of straight news journalism, gleefully seize any chance to involve themselves in documentary-making. Others are uncomfortable with the freedom on offer and are irritated by the comparative slowness of the production process, allied to the lack of editorial responsibility they may be given.

This is because the driving force is usually the producer, who is likely to spend several weeks researching a subject before a decision is taken whether to go ahead with it. The reporter may be brought in only at the tail-end to conduct prearranged interviews and to voice scripts written by other people, but how much involvement there is depends on the nature of the programme and its resources. Makers of series – even the most prestigious ones – are not necessarily assigned their own reporter, relying instead on presenters contracted programme by programme.

Documentary production

Documentary-making is usually altogether a more formal activity than 'news', a fact reflected in the size of the production team. Manning levels are laid down according to national or local management and union agreements, so a typical documentary team working on location might consist of six people, excluding the reporter, whose titles and responsibilities will vary accordinng to custom and practice.

The leader is probably the producer/director, who is in overall charge, combining the financial, editorial and creative responsibilities separated in feature film work. The production assistant may double as researcher as well as undertaking all detailed pre-production organisation, including making arrangements for the team's travel. On location she – as it usually is – keeps track of continuity, script and content. The camera operator works with the producer/director on the composition and framing of each shot, the business of handling the camera itself and loading the film being the responsibility of the assistant camera operator. In the same way, the sound recordist may have an assistant or second sound recordist to look after the equipment and 'slate' every shot with the clapperboard. Where necessary, the team is completed by an electrician, whose range and power of lights comfortably exceeds those used in news, and who may be joined by an assistant for particularly big or complicated productions.

Six stages in documentary-making

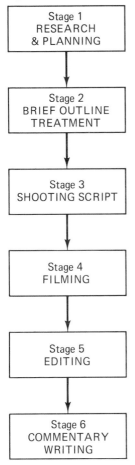

Documentary structure
Documentary-making calls for a disciplined approach: in some cases the shape, content and script are decided in detail in advance. The aim is to sustain interest throughout a film lasting anything from about fifteen minutes to an hour or more, and with careful planning it is possible to create peaks of interest at set intervals.

Using Film

Despite the essential convenience and mobility that video has brought to today's highly competitive world of electronic journalism, filmcraft continues to be practised in a few corners where speed is not a priority. Many documentaries are still shot on 35 mm or 16 mm film, which is preferred for its picture quality and the precision of manual film editing. It is also said by some picture editors that the physical handling of film enhances their creative instincts in a way which electronic editing does not.

Film technique
Before the lightweight video revolution of the late 1970s, the manufacturers of newsfilm had introduced a 16 mm cine equivalent of the amateur photographer's 35 mm colour transparency, an original positive for projection but without the need to print. Documentary makers, however, have tended to stick to the more conventional negative–positive process in which the first viewing is made from a print of the rushes – unedited raw material – and the original is stored under laboratory conditions to keep it free from dust, scratches or accidental mishandling during editing. Only after the rushes have been assembled, first into a rough cut and then into a final fine cut, is the original negative produced and edited exactly to match.

Sound
The most commonly used sound system in documentary filming is known as double system (otherwise separate magnetic) or synchronous sound (sync sound). Here the camera operator takes the pictures while the recordist captures the sound on a high-quality recorder using quarter-inch magnetic tape. Camera and recorder work separately but are linked electronically to maintain synchronism. In operation the start of each shot is indicated by use of a clapperboard, although sometimes it is more convenient to make the mark with an inverted 'end board'. Once filming is complete, the film is developed separately and the quarter-inch tape re-recorded onto a ferrous oxide surface.

Using video with film
Although they might have a preference for film, producers and directors often make practical use of electronic technology. Rushes are easily transferred to home video format for examination and review at leisure. In this way preliminary decisions about the shape and content can be made without wasting valuable operational resources. 'Off-line' editing, an intermediate assembly of the video sound and pictures, may also take place at this point, providing the picture editor with an accurate guide from which the original negative can be cut.

146

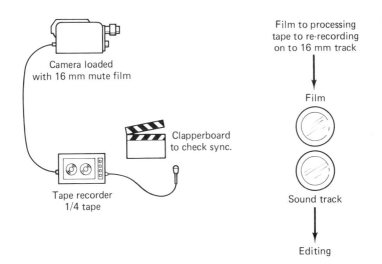

Camera loaded
with 16 mm mute film

Clapperboard
to check sync.

Tape recorder
1/4 tape

Film to processing
tape to re-recording
on to 16 mm track

Film

Sound track

Editing

Film sound
Many documentary makers use film in preference to videotape. The double system (also known as sync sound or sepmag) uses a separate tape machine to record the sound synchronously with the film.

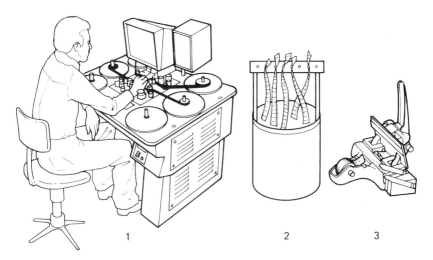

1   2   3

Film editing equipment
(1) Editing machine, (2) film bin on which the selected shots are pinned in sequence, and (3) the tape joiner. Cut film is butted together with transparent sticky tape.

Commentating

If you are blessed with a good voice and a gift for the right word, the time may come when you are pressed into service as a commentator on a special occasion. Commentating, a first cousin to reporting, is either live or recorded 'as live'. There is therefore no second chance to get things right, although in the latter case judicious editing of the sound track can spare some blushes. But it is never wise to assume that changes can be made.

First principles

The essence of good commentating for television is the conjunction of words and pictures. As with reporting, the commentator is there to complement what the viewer sees, but the difficulty lies in steering a path between useful information aiding comprehension and irritating irrelevance which does not. Planning is essential. Take advantage of the rehearsals for state occasions or other set-piece spectaculars, however sketchy they may be. Conduct your own on-the-spot reconnaissance. This, allied to thorough research, will make it possible to judge where it will be necessary to lighten the duller moments. The positive advantage is that you can expect to be out of shot during the performance, so full use can be made of a prepared script: you should be ready with a few important passages or detailed notes at the very least.

The bigger, or more international, the event the more likely you are to work in a booth with a monitor and lip microphone for company, well away from the action. All you see is what the viewer sees, the shot selected by the director from a multi-camera set-up. Your words should keep pace with the action, but if that is not possible it is far better to be ahead than behind by a few seconds. Don't allow yourself to be overawed by the occasion: keep the language simple and avoid pomposities.

Sport

Practically every sports fan reckons on being able to be as good if not a better commentator than those doing the job for a living. It is far more difficult than it seems. The more knowledgeable you are, the better: the less likely you will be to make the kind of mistakes which will have the aficionados calling for blood.

The secret is to know when to shut up, and let the action speak for itself. Some sports are obsessed with statistics, but opinion has it that the best commentary is one which confines itself to identification and interpretation, underpins the picture and avoids a stream of facts which get between the viewer and the game.

Guard against any tendency to treat sport less seriously than other subjects. In particular, don't patronise sportspeople by referring to them by their first names.

Commentating
It's important not to be overawed by the occasion. Keep the language simple and avoid pomposities. The bigger the event the more likely you are to be positioned in a booth some distance from the action (courtesy BBC Central Stills)

Whose Bias?

Unlike newspapers, whose editorial lines are frequently based on the political sympathies of their owners, many broadcast organisations are bound, morally or legally, to be impartial in their coverage of news, and to refrain from expressing opinions.

To those who suffer the excesses of the sillier side of the press (regrettably not confined to the tabloids) it comes as a relief to know that sanity is meant to prevail somewhere. But the difficulty you face as a television reporter is how to keep your audience fully informed about matters of a highly complex and political nature at the same time as maintaining a duty not to take sides.

A complication is the opinion of some in high places that a decision to cover an item is itself evidence of partiality. There is no comfort in knowing that bias is in the eye of the beholder, or that history has made a habit of blaming the messenger for the message. The question is how to square the circle.

Impartiality versus balance
It used to be believed that 'impartiality' was synonymous with 'balance'. This is no longer the case because 'balance' – implying equality – is not always strictly fair. Using a stopwatch to ensure that speech extracts from two opposing politicians are of the same duration may be doing both a disservice. One might be as effective in half the time. A perfect 'balance' which resulted in two sides cancelling each other out might be of no practical value and leave the audience none the wiser. As for 'impartiality', that is now seen as more of a doctrine than the definition of a single editorial principle.

Neutrality
Neutrality could be thought of as offering an alternative. But it is not possible to apply that stance to everything. There are moral absolutes about which it is impossible to remain neutral and civilised. Truth not lies; justice not injustice; freedom not slavery. Decent journalists are not neutral about racism or cruelty, but they are truthful about the facts of them.

Fairness
In the absence of anything else, the notion of fairness seems to be the most sensible. At least it has a positive ring to it. It also has the merit of flexibility. Fairness in one case may be to seek an interviewee's contribution 'live' rather than recorded. Fairness in a second way may be to paraphrase an interviewee's remarks. Fairness in a third may be to ask someone else.

150

Fairness guidelines

- *Tell potential interviewees why you want them.*

They have a right to know how you intend to use their contribution, and in what context. Be prepared to have your invitation declined.

- *Protect your sources.*

But be aware of the legal risks. In some circumstances refusal may lead to a fine or imprisonment.

- *Stick to the facts.*

Do not be tempted to speculate unless you possess information from which you can properly draw conclusions. If the opposition wants to 'take a flyer with the truth', let it.

- *Choose adjectives with care.*

They could be interpreted as 'editorialising'. Better still, avoid adjectives altogether. Well-written reports, accompanied by good pictures, rarely need embellishment.

- *Keep your opinions to yourself.*

It's unprofessional – and the audience is more interested in what your contributor has to say.

- *Avoid partiality.*

It's as wrong to champion the weak because they are weak as to favour the important or powerful.

- *Don't overcompensate.*

If you are not in personal sympathy with one argument, do not overcompensate with conscious bias towards the other.

- *Do not take advantage.*

People are not fair game because they are unfamiliar with the medium. Don't play the tricks of the trade.

- *Observe and report.*

You are bound to witness injustice. It is your job to observe and report it dispassionately. Let the audience draw their own conclusions.

- *Treat others as you would wish to be treated yourself.*

The Bounds of Good Taste

To any of the artificial satellites of the global communications network it makes no difference whether the television signals it beams from one side of the world to the other represent the most horrific pictures of a landslide in Columbia or the colourful frenzy of a Rio carnival. The geography and the technical operations remain the same.

Television reporters, like doctors, come across violence, death and human suffering as a normal part of their daily routine in a fast-moving and complicated world. Like doctors, they become inured to it all or cease to function effectively. The only way some reporters get through weary years of covering stories associated with terrorism or other violence is to grow a protective mental skin of indifference. Sometimes it becomes too thick. When that happens they recognise in themselves a lack of normal human response to each new atrocity and call a halt.

The viewer sitting at home has no inkling of the emotions of those involved in deciding how much of the cruel world can safely be shown.

The danger in your presence

In some situations the presence of you and your camera crew can inflame passions and lead to events which would not have occurred had you not been there to witness them. At all times be alive to the potential for manipulation, and avoid recording acts of violence that you suspect may be being staged for you. If in any doubt keep the camera out of sight.

Scenes of violence

When you do witness violent scenes, don't believe you are acting responsibly by including them in your coverage and expecting senior colleagues to decide whether to edit them out. You must judge for yourself whether they add to or subtract from the strength of your report.

Avoid lingering close-ups of pools of blood, bits of bodies, or whole bodies identifiable to relatives. Long shots can be just as effective.

Take account of who will be watching and when. Children or people viewing alone can easily be upset.

Your responsibility

Let none of these difficulties make you forget your responsibility for fair, honest reporting. Weigh that against the risk of offending the substantial lobby of opinion which would rather be left safely in ignorance of anything which is unsavoury or violent. These people have as much right to be considered as those who are voyeuristic or those who, out of genuine concern for their fellow humans, wish to be told the unsanitised truth, however much it hurts.

Violence: code of practice
The Broadcasting Standards Council, concerned chiefly with the portrayal of violence and sex and standards of taste and decency on television and radio, was set up by the government in Britain in 1988. A draft code was published in February 1989, followed by a revised version six months later after discussion with the broadcasting organisations. The sections on violence in news and and current affairs programmes are reproduced in full. Make up your own mind about their relevance.

BROADCASTING STANDARDS COUNCIL
A CODE OF PRACTICE [EXTRACT]

Violence in News and Current Affairs

1. *News Bulletins*
(a) *Television: The Raw Material*
   Modern communications make it possible for News bulletins to reflect almost instantly events taking place anywhere in the world. For some years, the raw material of coverage has been reaching newsrooms in abundance, whether it concerns a terrorist incident in Beirut, an attempt to rescue trapped whales from the Arctic ice, or a disastrous launch at Cape Canaveral. More recently, there has been a development in the supply of complete items packaged at a distant location, whether by the broadcasting organisation itself or by a news-gathering company wholly independent of it. Unified editorial control is increasingly impractical, with all the risks to standards which this implies. Broadcasting managements should therefore take special care to ensure that those exercising editorial judgements are aware of the principles which should underlie them. The supply of all-day news-services based on a rotating sequence of items, some repeated several times in succeeding cycles, is growing. Those responsible must pay close attention to each cycle to ensure the continuing suitability of the material and to guard against the possibility that repeated showings may breed indifference or revulsion.

(b) *Television: Pictorial Coverage*
   For the majority of people in Britain, the only acquaintance with real-life violence continues to be through the media, especially television. It is the media which bring them news of bombings in South Africa, motorway crashes in Britain, or the murder of hostages in the Middle East. It is not the business of the broad-

casters to falsify the picture of a world in which there is much violence and brutality. But in avoiding that trap, it is necessary to avoid falling into another which would leave the audience with an unjustified aggravation of any real threat to its own physical or mental security. For example, elderly people frightened about the consequences of venturing out of doors at night may develop an unreasoning fear about the real risks of doing so. The choice of words is a matter for the greatest care if they are to put into perspective the pictures which accompany them.

(c) *Television: Degrees of Explicitness*

Where scenes of violence are necessarily included in television bulletins, the fact that violence often has bloody consequences should not be glossed over. However, it is not for the broadcaster to force a moral judgement on the audience and care should be taken not to linger unwarrantably on the casualties nor on the bloody evidence of violence. Decency suggests that those who can should be permitted to die in private and only in the rarest circumstances should broadcasting linger on the moment of death itself. The repetition of such incidents in later broadcasts should be very restricted and their historical significance (for example, the assassination of President Kennedy) taken into account. A further relevant consideration is the nature of the programme for which the re-broadcast is proposed. Finally, telling the truth about an incident is the reporter's task, bringing home the truth is usually something better left for the audience to do for itself. It should not be forgotten that, for the audience, the too-vivid portrayal of violence can lead to revulsion rather than the communication of any truth about the incident portrayed.

(d) *Television: The Child Audience*

News bulletins are now part of the day-long output of many television services. At some times of the day, large numbers of children are present in the television audience or may be drawn to the screen by the pictures on it. There must continue to be discretion of the kind at present practised by the broadcasters in the choice of scenes at different times of day since images may have a disproportionate effect on children in comparison with words. A late-evening bulletin can be justified in carrying a greater degree of explicit violence than a bulletin in the early afternoon or evening. The question is not one of concealing the truth, since accompanying words can convey to the audience facts which, at that time of day, would be unacceptable pictorially. However, at any time, information accompanying pictures needs to be set in its proper context. Most violence has origins which can be explained, even when it cannot be defended.

(e) *Radio: General Considerations*

Although radio does not face the problems created by images for those responsible for television news coverage, it must still deal with the questions posed by the immediacy of its ability to respond to news-events, usually greater for radio than television, and the difficulty of maintaining a perspective on the violence it reports. A reporter's first choice of words may be crucial in influencing the public's understanding of an event, to which, where casualties occur, accurate reporting of their details may be equally so. In reporting certain kinds of crime, such as sexual assaults, the time of transmission must be considered and the degree of explicit detail given matched to the probable presence in the audience of significant numbers of children.

(f) *Violent Crime*

There are few crimes which are without their victims and nothing should be done which encourages the victims to be forgotten. Sexual violence or violence directed at older people, children, or people with disabilities should be reported with special understanding and an awareness of the time of day at which the bulletin is being transmitted. While in some cases, the victims of assault may be prepared to be interviewed, the degree of shock which they have recently experienced must be considered and no advantage taken of it.

(g) *Dealing with Violent Criminals*

In reporting crime involving violence, it is necessary to avoid glamourising the criminal or his actions. The use of nicknames for notorious criminals which may soften their image should be discouraged. The fact that, in fiction, some criminals can be made to cut romantic figures should not blind us to the ugliness of the real thing. A violent criminal under sentence, for example, remains one even if he succeeds in escaping from imprisonment. At the end of long criminal trials, it is not unusual for News bulletins to devote considerable stretches of time to reviewing the events leading to the prosecution. Such reviews should do nothing to present the defendants as heroic figures or as the stuff of legends. Neither criminals nor their relatives and associates should in general be allowed to profit from the retelling of their stories.

2. *Current Affairs and Documentaries*

(a) *General*

The principles governing the portrayal of violence which apply to the presentation of News apply to Current Affairs and Documentary programmes: including attention to the time of scheduling, no undue lingering on the aftermath of violent actions (but no glossing over the consequences of violence), and no incitement to or glorification of crime. The same caution called for in reporting in News bulletins certain kinds of violence is needed in less-immediately topical programmes. Though archival programmes form a rich and valuable contribution to television and radio programming, it should be borne in mind, when programmes are making use of historical material or material from the not-too-recent past, that attitudes change towards past events at different rates. The issue is as much one of Taste and Decency as it is of Violence. Although the spectacle of First World War troops going over the top to their deaths is still profoundly moving seventy years or more later, few people now remain with a direct personal involvement, either as a participant or a relative. But only twenty years have passed, for example, since the first showing on film of the street-execution of a Viet-Cong sympathiser and it remains a sickening spectacle for many people. The distraught commentary on the pre-war Hindenburg disaster continues to provide painful listening, while the explosion of the Challenger over Cape Canaveral, however spectacular, is still a living tragedy for many who witnessed it on television at the time it happened or immediately afterwards. In short, in drawing on a common stock of horrors for the purposes of illustration, care is necessary.

(b) *Reconstructions of Crime*

It is important, when restaging a crime as part of a programme aimed at assisting the police, not to give over-emphasis to the dramatic aspects of the incident, including any violence used, nor discuss in unnecessary detail the weapons employed.

Don't let your outside interests interfere with your job.

Other Codes of Conduct

Journalists, professional bodies, and employers in broadcasting and other parts of the media have for many years published their own guidelines, which are enshrined in office Style Books, Newsroom Guides and Professional Codes of Conduct. These are often intended to serve a dual purpose – to ensure stylistic consistency, including spelling and detailed use of language, and to establish ground-rules for ethical behaviour and editorial standards. Among these:

• The National Union of Journalists represents the majority of unionized journalists working in British broadcasting and the newspaper industry. Its code covers a wide range of conduct including professional and ethical standards, defence of press freedom, fairness, accuracy and the protection of sources.

• The BBC's Producers' Guidelines, which have been made available to the public as well as distributed to staff, establish a framework for ethical behaviour on straight dealing in programmes, impartiality, privacy, crime reporting, terrorism, taste and decency, violence and many other important issues.

• Britain's national newspaper editors agreed their own common code in 1989. Their recognition of the need for improved self-regulation is published under five main headings: Respect for Privacy, Opportunity for Reply, Prompt Correction, Conduct of Journalists, Race and Colour. They also agreed on the establishment of a system of readers' representatives to take up complaints and breaches of the code.

The *Post's* policy
In the United States, the respected *Washington Post* has pledged itself to strict avoidance of conflicting interests or the appearance of conflicting interests as part of a firm policy on standards and ethics. Reporters and editors must accept no free trips or gifts from news sources, and must not be actively involved in any partisan causes which could compromise the paper's ability to report and edit fairly. Invitations to meals are one of the few exceptions to the 'no gift' rule.

Commonsense rules
No-one wants to stop you playing a full part in society, but as a reporter you are inevitably in the public eye, and it is important to accept from the outset that your conduct – off-duty especially – could affect your credibility with the audience. My strong advice, old-fashioned though it might seem, is based on commonsense: avoid any interests which others might construe as being in conflict with your professional responsibilities.

The Oxygen of Publicity

The moral dilemma for television journalists in a modern society beset by political terrorism and violence is how to report responsibly without appearing to encourage the perpetrators through publicity.

In 1985, after Middle Eastern hijackers used the capture of an American jumbo jet aircraft to exploit the passengers and crew politically by making them appear at 'news conferences', Britain's Prime Minister, Margaret Thatcher, suggested that the media – television in particular – should deprive terrorists of what she called 'the oxygen of publicity'. She believed that restricting coverage of such acts might actually reduce them. Her plea for a voluntary code of conduct was sympathetically received but went unheeded. Three years later the running sore of trouble in Northern Ireland led to the introduction by her administration of a ban intended to keep the voices of terrorists and their apologists off the screen. If the journalists saw it as censorship, the public seemed largely indifferent.

The journalist's dilemma

The genuine, seemingly insoluble, problem this poses for a democratic society is how far those who are committed to destroying democracy should be given the opportunity to espouse ways of doing so. In the early 1960s, television occasionally allowed itself unwittingly to be manipulated by small, often unrepresentative groups, who cleverly chose to stage demonstrations – deliberately provoking police reaction – on traditionally quiet news days and at times and places which virtually guaranteed them maximum airtime. It was surprising how little trouble there was when the cameras were not there, and how few demonstrations there are now in comparison with those innocent days.

News blackouts

So how far should you co-operate with 'authority' to keep the 'oxygen of publicity' to a reasonable level? In Britain a voluntary code drawn up by representatives of broadcasting and the press and the police allows for a news blackout in kidnap cases where human life is thought to be seriously at stake.

The existence of any such agreements does not exempt reporters at 'the sharp end' from being alert to the legitimate needs of their profession and the public they serve. They should not allow themselves to be manipulated by those who would seek to manage the news to cover up their own shortcomings, or for some other purpose.

At the same time, as a reporter you do not stand apart from society, and ringing declarations about 'the freedom of the press' have a hollow sound to them when someone else's freedom – or life – is at risk.

158

The oxygen of publicity
Hijackings and other terrorist incidents have led to the deaths of many innocent people. Would it help if such events went unreported? (courtesy BBC Central Stills)

Investigative Journalism

The term 'investigative journalism' is one freely applied by many young reporters to what they regard as a romantic if rather shadowy side of the business. They see themselves uncovering wrongdoing and fearlessly exposing it. They have as an example the Watergate scandal and the part played by journalists – particularly Carl Bernstein and Bob Woodward of the Washington Post – in the eventual downfall of President Nixon in 1974.

But investigative journalism, conducted properly, is a time-consuming and expensive business. Newspapers which treat it seriously accept that it is a team effort, assigning researchers and reporters for weeks, perhaps months, swamping a subject from all sides to produce a mass of material from which the final article will appear.

The difficulty for television
Few but the very rich television news organisations can afford resources on a similar scale. Finding ways of illustrating abstract subjects can be extremely difficult if it is to be accurate as well as informative, and reporters and camera crews are not usually able to roam the world for months at a time in search of material for a project which might in the end turn out to be unproductive.

The need for care
All 'investigative' reports must be undertaken with scrupulous attention to accuracy. Above all it is essential to make sure there is something to investigate. Enthusiasm can blind even the most fair-minded to deficiencies in a potential story, and a misplaced sense of pride can allow the continued investigation of a subject which it is suspected, deep down, does not really 'stand up'. It is far better to cut and run at this stage, accepting that any money spent has been wasted, rather than press on with a report which would be unsatisfactory professionally or legally.

When a subject is worth pursuing, meticulous attention to detail is crucial. An otherwise well-constructed, thoughtful item can be undermined by the use of a few seconds of archive footage which gives the misleading impression that it is current. If legally sensitive issues are at stake, properly witnessed affidavits should be sought from interviewees. The advice of lawyers should be taken at all stages to avoid problems later on. All relevant documents should be filed and kept. The same applies to untransmitted film or video material.

In-depth reporting
'In-depth' reporting is usually synonymous with 'long'. Duration should have nothing to do with it, provided a subject is thoroughly researched and properly presented.

Journalists are not exempt from obeying the law.

Matters of Law (1)

It surprises some journalists to learn they are not above the law, and that somehow the words 'Press' or 'Television' do not magically bestow on them privileges denied to those engaged in more mundane occupations.

Their disappointment at this truism is then temporarily relieved by the genuine belief that at least they have carte blanche when working in countries other than their own, and that measures aimed at controlling the indigenous media do not apply to them. Regrettably they usually need to be convinced on that score, too – also to be reminded that leaving one 'hostile' country to find a friendlier one from which to file an 'illegal' report is a way round restrictions only as long as they have no intention of returning. Even despots watch television and listen to radio.

Legal obligations

No reporter is above the laws of the lands in which they operate. This may be inconvenient and it certainly may not square with your own conscience or preference for how society should operate. But there is no escaping your obligation to pursue your activities within the local legal system as it exists, whatever inadequacies it may contain. Until the system changes, you risk bringing down the full weight of the law upon yourself and being put out of business, imprisoned or expelled, and having equipment confiscated.

In rare cases the risk of incurring heavy penalties may be judged worthwhile, but at what stage it becomes desirable to flout the laws of some unpleasant foreign regime on a matter of principle depends on the value placed on the need to keep the doors of communication ajar.

South African restrictions

The South African Government's restrictions on the coverage of aspects of its internal troubles means that since the late 1980s representatives of the foreign press and broadcasting have been unable to report as freely as they would wish, but by operating within the restrictions they have at least been able to secure some coverage. At the same time the 'health warnings' accompanying reports have left the audience in no doubt about the difficulties under which news gathering has been carried out. This is far from ideal: it is also far more than could be achieved from a prison cell. The continuing presence of the international media allows public opinion to remain constantly aware of the problems which beset South Africa – unlike so many other countries, which might as well not exist for all the attention they allow themselves to receive.

Matters of Law (2)

The law can be something of a minefield, even for the experienced journalist. For the untrained newcomer it can be a nightmare. For those in between, a very sketchy knowledge can be the most dangerous of all.

A detailed examination of all the laws which affect journalists is obviously not within the scope of this book – specialist publications exist to meet that need (Greenwood and Welsh, for example: page 168). But an idea of the complexity of legal matters and the risks journalists run can be seen from an outline of the most relevant laws affecting British journalists.

Defamation

The law of defamation exists to protect the reputation of every individual from unjustified attack. It has two branches – slander, which broadly covers the spoken word, and libel, which broadly covers anything written or in other permanent form. A defamatory statement made in a television or radio broadcast would be classed as libel. The judge in such cases has to rule whether the words complained of are capable of having a defamatory meaning: it is up to the jury to decide whether they were defamatory.

Contempt of court

This covers reporting the progress of crime and the protection it affords the accused. Its aim is to ensure that every trial is conducted fairly and without prejudice, based on the assumption of innocence until guilt is proved. From the moment a case becomes 'active', journalists are limited in what they can report, and there are additional restrictions when cases involve juveniles, rape, and some other categories of crime.

Copyright and Official Secrets

Copyright exists to protect an author for his work. ('Authors' are artists, architects, composers, etc., as well as writers.) The Copyright, Designs and Patents Act 1988 also establishes the concept of 'moral rights'. Revisions to the Official Secrets Acts, the principal one of which was passed in 1911, were given the Royal Assent in 1989. The aim was to simplify the law, but the changes also did away with the 'public interest' defence to the controversial Section 2.

Other laws

Other laws affecting the work of journalists include confidentiality, which applies to the passing on of confidential information; the Race Relations Act; the Data Protection Act, which deals with computer data; and the Representation of the People Act, which lays down restrictions on the coverage of elections.

TV Reporting in the Year 2000

Before the end of the century the sweeping technological advances which have marked the development of television since the late 1970s will be serving the journalists of a new age.

By then, it is conceivable that a different kind of recruit will be joining the ranks, because the concept of the 'reporter' as merely an on-screen performer will be out of date, inadequate for the breadth of responsibility bestowed on someone who combines all the techniques and talents previously contributed by a whole team of technicians. The one-man/one woman band will be just that.

One-piece equipment
Of course, the 'stars' will remain, but duties will be interchangeable. As a matter of routine, every member of the news unit will be trained to shoot, view and edit their own material on a one-piece, lightweight cam-corder–editor, compose the script in the field on a portable computer patched through to home base giving access to a complete range of wire services. The same link will allow the new journalist to scour 'cuttings' from on-line library sources, create, select and retrieve images from digital stills and graphics stores, and to keep abreast of changes in programme rundowns/running orders.

Present-day video technology will have given away to cassette re-corders which do not use conventional tapes or have moving parts. The sound will be clean stereo, unimpaired by any editing, and the perfect piece to camera will be delivered, prompted by a laser-generated hologram.

To transmit the edited package, complete with graphics and automatic production instructions, all that will be necessary will be to unpack a miniature dish from your electrically powered car, contact base from almost anywhere in the world using a direct-dial cellular telephone, and bounce sound and pictures off any one of a skyful of orbiting satellites. Costs will be kept down by doubling or tripling the transmission speed of the signals, which will then be recorded and 'stretched' for replaying normally at the other end.

In the unlikely event of having to return to base, the new journalist will appear in a studio in front of robot cameras programmed by a solitary technician in the studio transmission suite, graphics and video inserts controlled by instructions buried within scripts composed on the news-room computer.

Back at home after a hard day's work, the new journalist will relax in front of a wall-hung, wafer-thin television screen giving brilliant definition through more than one thousand lines. Details of *tomorrow's* assignment await the touch of a button on the computer.

A bumpy ride?

The Future of TV Journalism

No-one can predict how many convulsions television's newest revolution will have to go through before cable and satellite services are finally established as part of the fabric of global broadcasting. On the evidence of the difficulties which beset the pioneering efforts of Europa Television and Super Channel in the late 1980s we are in for a bumpy ride.

The danger for journalism
Like it or not, though, television journalism cannot expect to remain unaffected by any battle fought over the necessity to deliver audiences to advertisers. The danger is that to survive in a competitive commercial environment – one in which, to put it crudely, the audience has an increasingly attractive invitation to switch channels – it could be forced downmarket towards its own version of the kind of journalism provided by much of the tabloid press.

This is sometimes euphemistically described as 'giving the public what it wants', at face value a laudable enough aim, but all too often an excuse for abandoning the reporting of the more difficult and complex issues in favour of 'infotainment', a chiefly home-story led mishmash of frothy contrivances. Television journalism is of no value to anyone if it is reduced to flashy graphics and a series of meaningless, 15-second bites at the end of which the viewer's response amounts to 'so what?'

And here the advance of new technology is a positive disadvantage. Because virtually anyone with a video camera is able to shoot acceptable pictures under almost any conditions, the hard-nosed editorial professionalism which now prevails will give way to the philosophy which puts its trust in anything that moves and can be labelled 'live' or 'exclusive'.

Alongside this is a tendency to denigrate television journalism as a craft in the belief that it is no more than radio with pictures, and as such requires no special technique. The result, already apparent alas, can be seen in the performances of some reporters who have not been fully prepared for their role.

The impetus for change
On the brighter side, more television journalism does not have to mean poorer quality: on the contrary, if the intensity of competition forces the present generation of television journalists to expand the news agenda and leads to the examination of new issues or better treatment of old ones, the public as a whole will be better served than before.

A final word of caution. Recruitment of the brightest and best young minds into television brings with it the responsibility to provide the best possible training, allied to the old-fashioned virtues of accuracy and fairness. Only if those who run the programmes are not deflected from their determination to maintain high standards will the integrity of television reporting remain intact.

164

Glossary

Anchor Chief presenter of a programme. Alternatively *Newscaster, Newsreader, Presenter.*

Archive material Library or file footage.

Associate/assistant producer Newsroom journalist/writer responsible for shaping individual items for programmes. May have some reporting duties.

Assignments editors Assigners of reporters and camera crews to events for coverage.

Assignment sheet Information about an event to be covered.

Betacam Half-inch ENG video format introduced by Sony.

Bird Communications satellite named after Early Bird, the first satellite launched by *Intelsat*, the International Television Satellite Organisation.

Camcorder Combined video camera and cassette recorder.

Cans Earphones.

Ceefax Broadcast teletext system.

Character generator Electronic method of producing on-screen lettering.

Clipping/cutting Item copied or cut from a newspaper or other printed source.

Communications satellite Space device for transmitting sound and picture signals over long distances.

Control room Technical area from which studio production is controlled.

Copy Written material for news.

Correspondent Specialist senior reporter.

Count down Reporter's studio aid. Time given in reverse order to ensure the smooth transition from one source to the next.

Cu Close-up.

Cue Signal given to start or stop action.

Cutaway/in Reporter's questions repeated for the camera after interview to provide continuity between edited sections.

Cut story Edited news picture item.

DBS Direct Broadcasting by Satellite. System for broadcasting television to individual home by satellite.

Deaf aid Earpiece through which a reporter can be given instructions.

Diary story News event covered by prearrangement.

Dish Antenna for receiving or transmitting satellite and microwave signals.

Door-stepper Interview obtained by waiting for the subject 'on the doorstep'.

Dry run Rehearsal without the camera.

Dub To add or re-record sound to edited pictures.

Duration Length in time of a programme or item.

Editor Senior executive in charge of a news programme.

Eng Electronic News Gathering. Lightweight video camera and sound recording system.

Establishing shot Scene-setting shot of people or subject.

Eye-line Direction in which the subject is seen to be looking.

Field producer Editorial supervisor of assignment off base. Also *Fixer*.

File Send a report.

Fire brigade Editorial/camera team assigned at short notice to cover news breaks, usually abroad.

Fixer Editorial co-ordinator accompanying reporters in the field.

Follow-up Report based on previously broadcast or published material.

Format Programme style.

Futures Details of items for possible future news coverage.

Graphics Television artwork.

Gun mike See *Rifle mike*.

GV General View.

Hard news 'Straight' news.

In-cue Opening words of a news report.

Intake/input Department responsible for arranging news gathering.

Intro(duction) First sentence of a news story.

Jump cut Edit interrupting pictorial continuity. The subject appears to jump from one position to another in consecutive shots.

Lead-in Introduction.

Live In real time.

Location Geographical position of an event.

LS Long shot.

Mic/mike Microphone.

Minicam Mobile electronic camera unit with live capability.

Monitor Electronic display screen.

Natural sound The sound of reality.

Neck/personal mike Lightweight microphone fixed to a neck cord or clipped onto clothing.

News director (US) Executive in charge of news department.

News editor Senior journalist usually concerned with news gathering.

Newswriter Newsroom-based journalist responsible for assembling and writing programme items.

Noddies Simulated reaction shots for use as interview cut-aways.

OC On camera.

Oracle Optional Reception of Announcements by Coded Line Electronics. Broadcast teletext.

Out cue Closing words of a news report.

Output Department responsible for selecting and processing news material for transmission.

Out-takes Recorded unused material.

Package Reporter's self-contained item combining several different elements.

Pan Camera movement horizontally or vertically.

Producer Person responsible for entire programme or item within it.

Radio mike Microphone with small transmitter. Needs no cable link with recording equipment.

Rifle mike Microphone with rifle-shaped barrel.

Rough cut First assembly of tape or film edited to its approximately pre-selected duration and shape.

Running order/rundown Order of transmission of items in a programme.

Run through Rehearsal.

Run up Time necessary for technical equipment to reach its operating speed.

Rushes (dailies) Unedited material.

Sync sound Film sound recording system. The sound is recorded on to tape synchronously with the film.

Shot list Means by which commentary is made to match pictures from detailed description of what each shot contains.

Sound bite Sound, usually speech, extract chosen for inclusion in news package.

Stand-up (per)/piece to camera Report spoken directly to the camera in the field.

Stick mike Stick-shaped microphone commonly used in news work.

Stringer Freelance journalist contributor employed on a regular basis.

Talk-back One-way sound link between control room and other technical area.

Talking head Any interviewee.

Teletext Broadcast videotex. Appears on television screen as written text.

Tilt Vertical panning camera movement.

Tripod Three-legged stand fixed to the base of a camera to keep it steady.

Two-shot A shot of two people.

Tx Transmission.

U-matic Three-quarter inch videotape recording system.

Upcut Accidental overlapping of two sound sources.

Videotape (VT/VTR) Electronic recording system for sound and pictures.

Video (tape) cassette Tape container for cameras and recorders.

Voice-over Off-camera commentary.

Vox pops Random interviews edited to give a cross-section of opinion.

Wire copy Written material received from news agency sources.

Further Reading

A *Code of Practice* (draft), Broadcasting Standards Council, 1989
A *Style Guide*, BBC, 1988
A *Way with Words*, by John Behague, Brighton Polytechnic, 1984
Broadcast Journalism, by Andrew Boyd, Heinemann Professional Publishing, 1988
Dictionary of Eponyms, by Martin Manser, Sphere, 1988
Essential Law for Journalists (10th edition), by Walter Greenwood and Tom Welsh, Butterworths, 1988
Journalists on Dangerous Assignments, edited by Louis Falls Montgomery, International Press Institute, 1986
Journalists at War, by David E. Morrison and Howard Tumber, Sage Publications, 1988
Now the News in Detail, by Murray Masterson and Roger Patching, Deakin University Press, 1986
Producers' Guidelines, BBC, 1989
Pronouncing Dictionary of British Names, BBC, 1983
The Handbook of Non-Sexist Writing, by Casey Miller and Kate Swift, The Women's Press, 1989
The Technique of Television News, by Ivor Yorke, Focal Press, 1987
The Voice Book, by Michael McCallion, Faber and Faber, 1988
Troublesome Words, by Bill Bryson, Penguin, 1988
TV News: building a career in broadcast journalism, by Ray White, Focal Press, 1990
TV News Off-Camera, by Steven Zousmer, The University of Michigan Press, 1987